The Challenge is a beautiful story of one young man's journey from being lost and then found. The reader will experience the emotions and pain of both a father and a son, as they exchange heartfelt letters to each other and, in the end, discover 'The Prize" they have been seeking.

> Kary Oberbrunner, Author of *Elixir Project* and *Day Job to Dream Job*

Author Jim Mazziotti was at his wits end. He was losing his son who was in the process of throwing away his life, and help seemed nonexistent. Then Jim found a boarding school that would change both their lives. The heartrendingly candid and inspiring 144 letters Jim wrote his son over the course of 5 1/2 months would help his son overcome 'The Challenge' and grow into the man his father always knew he could be. A father-son love story you won't want to miss.

> Linden Gross - One Stop Writing Shop

The depth of a father's love has the power to change lives and the course of history. There is something magical about a father's love that draws us to it—we thirst for its redemptive blessing. Love wins if we cling to it, learn from it and apply it. Jim Mazziotti takes you on a journey in *The Challenge* that will raise your faith in the power and source of love.

> Jim Akers
> Author of Amazon #1 New Release
> *Tape Breakers:*
> *Maximize Your Impact With People You Love,*
> *Teams You Lead, and Causes that Stir Your Heart*

The Challenge is a fascinating and moving story of how simple handwritten letters connected a father and a son. You will be inspired. You will most certainly cry, and you will discover how one boy found the confidence to do anything! To my friend and fellow author, Jim Mazziotti, well done. This book and your life are truly an inspiration to me.

Scott Ballard
Coach, Author & Speaker
Confidence Coach LLC

THE CHALLENGE

THE CHALLENGE

How 144 Letters Changed My Life, The Life of My Son, And Will Change Your Life Too

Jim Mazziotti

AUTHOR ACADEMY elite

In order to maintain their anonymity and to protect the privacy of subjects in this story, I have changed the names of some individuals and places. I may have changed some identifying characteristics and details such as physical properties and occupations. I have tried to recreate events, locales, and conversations from my memories of them. The author and publisher have made every effort to ensure that the information in this book is correct. The author and publisher do not assume and hereby disclaim any liability to any party for any loss, damage, mischaracterization, or disruption caused by errors or omissions, whether such errors or omissions result from negligence, accident, or any other cause.

Copyright @2018 Jim Mazziotti
All rights reserved
Printed in the United States of America

Published by Author Academy Elite
P. O. Box 43, Powell, OH 43035
www.AuthorAcademyElite.com

All rights reserved.
No part of this publication may be reproduced, stored in a retrieval system, or transmitted in any form or by any means – for example, electronic, photocopy, recording, scanning – without the prior written permission of the publisher. The only exception is brief quotations in printed reviews.

Paperback ISBN: 978-1-64085-317-1
Hardcover ISBN: 978-1-64085-318-8
Ebook ISBN: 978-1-64085-319-5
Library of Congress Control Number: 2018943565

Cover design by Debbie O'Byrne
Development Editor: Michele Stanford
Interior Design by JetLaunch, Inc.

Any Internet or product information printed in this book is accurate at the time of publication. They are provided as a resource with the understanding content or permanence may change. Jim Mazziotti or the publisher do not vouch for their content or permanence.

The Challenge: How 144 Letters Changed My Life, The Life Of My Son, And Will Change Your Life Too is available at special quantity discounts to use as premiums and sales promotions, for schools, or for use in corporate training programs. For more information contact the author directly

Dedication

To Tony

In his book *Remembering Isaac: The Wise and Joyful Potter of Niederbipp*, Ben Behunin said, "There is more to a boy than what his mother sees. There is more to a boy than what his father dreams. Inside every boy lies a heart that beats. And sometimes it screams, refusing to take defeat. And sometimes his father's dreams aren't big enough, and sometimes his mother's vision isn't long enough. And sometimes the boy has to dream his own dreams and break through the clouds with his own sunbeams."

This book is dedicated to my first son, the first grandson to my father, Samuel J. Mazziotti. Dedicated to a boy who felt, perhaps, that dreams were meant for other people. To a boy who God gave so much and continues to give, and my hoping God's gifts are realized, accepted, and honored. To a boy who is now a man, and still, and always, my first son. Break through the clouds, Tony. Break through the clouds.

CONTENTS

Quote..xi

Foreword..xiii

Preface... xv

Introduction.. xxi

Chapter 1   The Beginning of The End: Sophomore Struggles..1

Chapter 2   Tony's Junior-Year Tailspin.............................15

Chapter 3   Tony's Short-Lived Alternative Success...........24

Chapter 4   Looking for a Way Out...................................31

Chapter 5   The Darkest Hour..41

Chapter 6   Orientation...50

Chapter 7   Accepted!..60

Chapter 8   "I'll Be Right Back…I Will See You in a Little While".......................................68

Chapter 9   The First of Our 144 Letters..........................79

Chapter 10   The Promise 86

Chapter 11	The Letters	98
Chapter 12	The Prospect of Success	108
Chapter 13	"Dad, I'm Going to Succeed"	123
Chapter 14	Going for Impact	131
Chapter 15	Tony's First Visit Home	144
Chapter 16	Law of the Lid	158
Chapter 17	Helping to Shape My Son's Life	166
Chapter 18	A Perfect Day	176
Chapter 19	A Thanksgiving of Mixed Feelings	185
Chapter 20	The 10 Things	198
Chapter 21	The Prize	207
Chapter 22	Graduation Day	216
Chapter 23	Afterword	224
Final Thoughts		229
Acknowledgments		233

Whether or not you write well, write bravely.

Bill Stout

FOREWORD

I have had the good fortune of knowing Jim Mazziotti (or Mazz as he is known to a special group of family and friends) since 2006. I met him before he purchased his EXIT Realty Bend franchise while he was investigating the opportunity. I remember instantly feeling that he "fit in." I came to learn that he has been focused on personal growth and development for a long time, which is one of the core philosophies of EXIT Realty. Jim has always been passionate about the well-being of his family and his agents as well as his duty as a servant leader.

Jim opened his EXIT Realty franchise in 2006, a little more than a year before the recession hit and his market took a downturn. He was challenged at work and at home. His investment in both money and love was at an all-time high. His concern for his children's future and the future of his business were keeping him up at night. As a parent and the leader of a company myself, I can empathize with those concerns. We second guess ourselves and feel overwhelmed from every angle; but, like the true leader he is, Jim remained focused on what he wanted the end result to be.

Jim takes personal pride in his heritage and expects his family to honor it. The decision to send his troubled son away for five and a half months and figure out a way to have his son "hear" his expressions of love without being able to see him, inspired Jim's letters. Muscles break down during exercise to rebuild stronger. I believe emotional and mental muscles have the same capacity when tested, and when done right, character and love prevail. Jim decided to write his son a letter every day and he committed to it. His heart knew it was the right way to break through. Their journey will touch your heart, it will inspire you to be a better parent and a better leader. The letters are a legacy for the Mazziotti family for generations to come.

I believe the ripple effect of this beautiful book will stretch much further than Jim could ever imagine. Escaping into a book and feeling the author's story can be an incredible journey; doing something better with your own life because of it is magic.

Thank you, Mazz, for this gift to all who will read it.

Tami Bonnell, CEO
EXIT Realty Corp. International

PREFACE

Our dreams are made of real things like a shoebox full of photographs.

Jack Johnson
American Musician

I wandered up to his room to sit and reminisce. We had kept Tony's room intact while he was away. Team pictures, blue ribbons, trophies, certificates, posters and multitudinous mementos covered the walls of his room. As I sat on his bed, I wondered how Leann and I might approach his room in the coming weeks; I mean, he would be gone from home for a long time. Of course, a single day seems a long time to be away from him. You know the feeling, right?

As I took it all in, I tried to remember when and where the pictures had been taken and his prized trophies won. I realized I didn't have clear memories of many of the photos or friends in the photographs. Time challenges our memory, surely; but it appeared from the evidence before me that much of his life had passed by without my taking notice. The human element of taking things for granted, I guess.

I approached his closet; it contained those things you might expect to find, arranged as only a teenage boy would care to have it. There were clothes on hangers. *Good job, Tony.*

There were clothes stuffed on shelves, the floor, and behind storage bins containing baseball cards and old toys that had long ago been retired. I reached into a box and grabbed one of the hundreds of match-box die-cast cars. I remembered, when he was just a little boy, how I would bring home a new car for him that I would purchase at the Ertl Toy Store in Dyersville, Iowa, or just about any toy store I could find when I was on the road selling musical instruments for our family music business. He would be waiting for me at the door when I arrived home and as I sat on the edge of his bed, I could visualize his beautiful little face, a smile from ear-to-ear, and his high-pitched voice.

And then, on the top shelf, all the way to the right side and below some caps and a baseball glove were the letters. Our letters.

The letters I had written to Tony were all placed neatly in a shoebox. It was a typical shoebox, I guess. It had a dark gray lid while the sides and bottom were a lighter gray, maybe like the gray you would see on a cool and crisp rainy day. Most of the letters were still in their original envelopes. I recognized some of the envelopes and I remember specifically writing on the outside of some of the them, something I did often, as if I had to get one more word in before placing the letters in the mailbox.

Looking at my letters reminded me of how deeply sad I was while writing so many of them. I could feel the sadness return as I ran my fingers over each one, attentively looking for clues that might remind me of the day I wrote the letters and the sadness that was part of almost every day that Tony was away. Interspersed with the letters I had written to Tony were letters and cards he had received from others as well. I never knew, or perhaps I had just forgotten, that so many people had also been part of the journey with Tony. All in all, there were more than 225 cards or letters that came home with Tony and that were placed into the old shoebox.

For thousands of years, letters have served as the primary connection between people. I've enjoyed reading published letters that now provide us with historic perspective and relevance to the way people have communicated with each other for centuries. The letters written by Dwight Eisenhower to his wife are some of my favorite, beautifully written letters.

Now, the letters written from me to Tony perhaps compare not to those written by Dwight Eisenhower to his wife, Mamie, in 1945 while fighting on the front lines during WWII, where one letter said, "Possibly I've been remiss about writing the past two weeks, although I've sent two or three teletypes. From my papers, you will understand that we have been under some stress, and you'll understand that it has been hard to sit down and to compose thoughts applicable to a letter to one's best only girl. . ." Or perhaps like one hand-written and undated from Marilyn Monroe to her famed acting teacher, Lee Strasberg, in which she sadly exclaimed, "… my will is weak, but I can't stand anything. I sound crazy, but I think I'm going crazy." Nor do our letters compare to any of the more than 250 letters and documents that were auctioned off by an anonymous collector in April of 2013 at the Douglas Elliman Madison Avenue Art Gallery.

However, the letters written from me to Tony and those written from him to me were special letters indeed. They weren't just special, they were "our letters." They will always be our letters. Letters that I am convinced changed our lives and might change your life too.

I have estimated that the time spent writing letters to Tony, while he was away for the five and a half- month period, was well over 300 hours. Easily. As I examined those 300 hours of preparing and writing the letters, I realized that it amounted to seven and a half 40-hour work weeks during this five-month period. Think about this: almost two months of what is considered full time employment was spent in writing letters!

I find it astonishing now that I look back on that time. During the time Tony spent away from home and in the Oregon Youth ChalleNGe facility, two things occupied almost my every thought: one, how can I help my son make it through one of the most intense alternative schools in the country; and two, how on earth will my real estate business survive in the worst housing market since the Great Depression? God help me if our economy, and specifically the housing market, takes 10 years to turn around. I didn't have ten years to languish in a devastated real estate market, and I, as sure as the sun rises each day, didn't have many more chances to help my son change his direction.

While I won't share each letter in this book, I will share those that Tony told me gave him the most hope, the most spiritual support, and the most optimism while spending his senior year in high school at the Oregon Youth ChalleNGe. I will also share passages from some of his letters. Picture where I might have been sitting or standing when writing my letters to Tony and what must have been going through his mind as he read them. I am guessing you will feel his pain, his joy, and his loneliness....and mine.

Sure, I wrote about the ordinary things of everyday life, but for me it was a question of how am I going to use my words to empower Tony? What can I say to help him, to empower him to find and to realize his potential? How do I help a lost young man discover his passion? What words will help him grow, address his flaws, focus on his strengths, and see his purpose? And most of all, how could I help him develop a strong character? Indeed, how could I shape my letters to be more than ordinary?

My mentor, John C. Maxwell, says that "Adversity writes our story, and if our response is right, the story will be good. Adversity without triumph is not inspiring; it's depressing. Adversity without growth is not encouraging; it's discouraging.

Adversity can create a story of hope and success." And that is exactly why I must write this book.

This is the story about my son, Tony, and how the letters I wrote to him each day changed his life and mine and I believe might change your life as well. His journey from an almost sure failure in life must be told in order to, at the very least, give hope to those parents and kids who think there is little hope in finding success. You will soon discover how the successes of our extraordinary journeys in life are attainable. Never easy, but attainable. I believe this story is inspiring and yes, there is plenty of hope and success within the pages of this book. I have told him, many times, and I say to you, just because your past may have been hard doesn't mean that your future can't be incredible.

INTRODUCTION

The Ultimatum Oh No...Oh No...Oh No!

MARCH 13, 2007

The end of a long, tedious and almost hopeless school year, his junior year, was about to end for Tony. It was Thursday. For the better part of seven months, we had dealt, almost daily, with the fact that Tony would take one step forward and he would find a way to take two steps back. Honestly, that is being much too kind in describing the reality of the direction his life was headed.

During this school year, we had chosen to remove Tony from Mountain View High School and enroll him in another school. This school, the Central Oregon Intergovernmental Council Alternative School (COIC) provided a precisely crafted alternative to his traditional high school; but honestly, it isn't a place where anyone aspires to be or where I see participants using it as a springboard to greatness. However, it gave Tony, and others, the ability to attend classes in a classroom each morning and the opportunity to study and to work outdoors in the afternoons. The outdoor experience allowed him to escape the stifling walls of a building and encounter learning in a way much different from the norm. Tony spent many of his afternoons in some of the most pristine and beautiful forests in the Pacific Northwest, if not the world. He worked with his hands and studied along rivers and beneath ancient trees. Still, this wasn't enough.

Over the previous two weeks Tony had been difficult. He was arriving home well after his curfew, hanging with the wrong crowd, and spending time with a girl who was nothing but trouble. We could see it. He did not. We were frustrated and by we, I mean my wife, Leann, our two kids, and me.

Nicole, our oldest child, then 23 years old, had little time for Tony's behavior. Christiano, our youngest, who was 12, most often just kept quiet, took it all in, and steered clear of the conversations between Tony and me. The environment at home was not the warm and nurturing place that it should have been nor what we desired it to be, for sure. It was more of a home filled with uneasiness and the prospect that something would surely go wrong on any given day. You know the feeling – the feeling that when the phone rings or the doorbell chimes bad news will come with it. Nicole, was still living at home having just graduated from college and was looking for her first teaching position in Central Oregon. She regularly took part in the conversations between Leann and me, always looking for the ways to move Tony from this place of failure. None were to be found. Not at this time, anyway.

Tony had gone out for the night – out meaning that either one of his friends or his girlfriend had picked him up to go somewhere. Tony still did not have a driver's license. The rule of our house was that driving a car required a B average in school. Tony had long ago given up any hope of convincing me otherwise. He knew better than to discuss alternatives because he knew there was no alternative to getting the grades. Period. The rule was laid down. Plain and simple. In fact, I cannot remember one instance where he pleaded, begged, or showed any anger about the rule. Not once. I'm not so sure I would have been as accepting of such a rule when I was his age. I can't imagine not spending time driving a car and cruising the strip with my buddies (and girls of course) when I was his age. Not having an automobile never seemed to prevent him from going where he wanted to go. All of his friends had cars. He was able to get to wherever he needed to go.

On this evening, a school night, he was to be by home at 10:00 p.m. No ifs, no ands, and no buts. Before he left for the evening, I made sure he understood that not arriving home by 10:00 p.m. would result in consequences. He had no idea what he was in for should he arrive home late on this night. Leann, Nicole, and myself had already decided the consequences should he not act accordingly. Christiano also knew of the ramifications.

Ten o'clock had arrived; and I knew it would, on this night, as sure as anything. I was exhausted and I anticipated that on this night our lives, our entire family's life would be changed forever. As the minutes passed, my stomach became more hollow and empty, not from hunger, but from disappointment, anger, fear, sadness, and hopelessness. Tonight, I had reached the end of my rope. Leann, Nicole, Christiano, and I knew we had to see this through, once and for all.

Ten o'clock turned to eleven o'clock and then to midnight. No phone call. No text message. I was checking to see if, for whatever reason, he would have chosen to email his mother or me. Not a word. As the clock ticked, the gap was widening between my sorrow and my anger. I thought through what I would say to him, how I would say it, and even where I would be sitting when he walked in the door. I knew I wanted to be collected, reasonable, but firm and direct. I practiced what I would say to him dozens of times in my head, nervously, restlessly; and each minute that passed made it more dreadful. How could I feel any worse? With each passing minute, I did.

I knew it was unlikely that Tony, upon walking in the house, would show any anger when I asked him to sit down and discuss our family decision. Tony was never directly disrespectful or argumentative to either his mother or me.

Never. Maybe he was just too tired of it all, the flailing and the thrashing, trying to find a way out of the hole he had fallen in. *God almighty.* The frustration Tony must have felt that would surely drive many kids off the cliff of desperation, despair, and despondency.

What is constantly going through his head, I contemplated. *Jesus Christ, I love him so much.* Will this be the right thing for him? Will I be offering him a way to finally find himself and his purpose? I thought of my father and what he might do. How he might handle this situation. Most certainly he had his own challenges with me, but nothing like this.

At 1:11 a.m. a car pulled up in front of the house. There was no mistaking it might be someone else at this time in the morning. Occasionally our neighbors across the street would call Dominos to deliver a pizza at this hour of the morning, but it was Tony. My gut churned and tightened. All of us, even Christiano, were sitting in the living room waiting for him. It was almost like the gathering of a family on some intervention show. I thought how ridiculous this was, but also how necessary.

Before the car door opened, Leann reminded me to keep calm and to control my emotions. She sat next to me, holding my hand; but, I was numb. My heart was palpitating like a hammer inside my chest. I don't remember feeling anything other than emotions ripping through me and second-guessing the screaming coming from somewhere inside of my head. Nicole encouraged, "It's okay Dad…you are doing the right thing." Christiano sat quietly. I knew he feared this moment, nervous for the outcome. *This wouldn't be happening in a normal family. What the hell is a normal family, anyway?*

The car door slammed. At that moment, I closed my eyes and offered up a quick prayer asking God to help me say the right things. Tony opened the front door at 1:13 a.m. I know this because the clock in our house hangs on the wall to the left of the front door and I was watching it intently. As Tony stepped foot inside, he could see my eyes focused on the clock and then him. I knew he saw that I was looking at the clock. He also looked at the four of us all sitting up and waiting for him. Our early morning gathering must have appeared like the worst surprise party he had ever imagined and maybe something closer to what George Custer experienced at Little Big Horn. In that moment, he knew. I could see that he knew this was not going to be a pleasant experience.

"What's up?" he asked all of us. He then looked toward his little brother and said, "Christiano, you have school tomorrow, what are you doing still up?"

It was at that moment my anger subsided. In this kind of situation, I would most often keep a stiff upper lip which often concealed clinched teeth; but at that moment I knew that to take meaningful action, I would need to keep my wits about me. As I looked at him standing there, I realized that my oldest son was about to see his life change in a matter of seconds. Change like he could never have imaged. He might as well have been 10 years old as I looked at him. Sure, he was standing at 6'4" and probably 175 pounds, but all I could see was a little boy in *big* trouble. Was this hopeless? I questioned. If I wanted to connect with him in a positive way, now was the time. Was I up to it?

In that instant, I realized what was about to happen would have a lasting impression on all of us. I decided to handle this situation calmly and rationally, or as close to it as I could possibly get. I have a fiery temper, but I was determined to turn the volume down (actually seeing a volume button in my head) and push the calm button. I wanted for my family, especially Christiano, to see how a very difficult situation could be handled with toughness; I mean, my kids will tell you that I have been a tough dad. I know that; but tonight, I wanted to show more than toughness. I wanted my entire family, especially my two boys, to witness their father handling a difficult situation with compassion, love, understanding, and empathy.

Recently I read an article in the Wall Street Journal written by Dave Shiflett where he spoke about his family's experience in caring for his father and mother in their time of decline and eventual death. In the article, he said, "We were reminded, vividly, that we are often at our best when life is at its worst." I guess that is how I might describe that early morning sitting with my family and knowing I was about to embark upon a huge alteration in Tony's life and that of our family and hoping I might be at my best.

"Sit down, Tony," I said to him.

"Okay, but what is everybody doing up? What is going on?"

"Tony, just sit down," I stated for a second time.

Tony moved quickly to an empty spot on the couch clearly uncomfortable by what was happening and not knowing exactly what was about to transpire

"Tony," I said calmly, "here is the situation. For weeks, we have seen your circumstances in school almost disintegrate before our eyes. You know what I am talking about?"

He shook his head up and down very quickly while sounding a "Uh huh" with his mouth closed with only the sound coming from his throat.

"Tony, for the past week all of us have been trying to figure out how we can help you get on the right track. Here is what we know. First, we all love you more than you can possibly imagine. Right now, at this very moment, we all hurt because we want to help you and haven't known how. You know that your mother and I have spent hours fighting for you at your school. You have witnessed a school counselor who, when we went for your scheduled appointment a few months ago, didn't even remember that she was your counselor. She actually thought you were a new incoming student, remember? The one person who should be looking out for you at your school abandoned you. You also know that promises and assurances that I received from the administration were never acted upon and that the help they promised to get you with your academics, beginning with state testing, never happened. Right?

"Most concerning tonight is that we all know your behavior in school has taken a turn for the worst. Tony, the gap is widening. We see you flailing. You put up a good front, but we can clearly see you suffering. God Tony! You must be exhausted! I know you well enough to see you are exhausted and exasperated and would quit school if we would allow you to do so. But you can't. You just can't! You know we believe that your relationships with those you have chosen to run with have not raised you up, but are quickly taking you down. Coming home at this hour tonight and for numerous nights is not acceptable. Plain and simple. You know that, don't you?" I said.

Tony again responded with an "uh huh!"

The tension filled the room. Tears were flowing out of the eyes of everyone, including mine.

My throat closed as I spoke. It was as if someone had their hands around my neck, pressing vigorously to prevent me from breathing. Tony looked almost helpless. Defenseless. Beaten. Defeated. He, too, had tears flowing down the left side of his face and his nose began to run. He stood and walked over to the coffee table and grabbed a Kleenex. Leann and Nici had already prepared by having some in their hands. Christiano, like most 12-year-olds chose to use the back of his hand, wiping the tears on his pant leg.

It was dead still at this time of the morning as the clock approached 2:00 a.m. It was very cool outside, but the inside of our home, even without the fireplace or heat turned on seemed too hot, perhaps from the blood and the adrenalin moving briskly through my body. Leann and Nicole added their thoughts which allowed me time to gather myself. Tony said nothing, only acknowledging what was said. He knew something was about to happen. I know it. He just knew.

Then the ultimatum.

"Tony, you have told us that you want to quit school and that there is no reason for you continuing to attend classes and that it is likely you won't be able to graduate," I said. "Here is what you need to know…" I positioned myself closer to him and with a monotone and firm voice said, "…MAZZIOTTI'S DO NOT QUIT OR DROP OUT OF SCHOOL. Period!"

There was no forgetting how I drove the point home to him. I wanted to be sure he heard me.

"Tony," I said, "You know me well enough to know that this is not open for discussion." I looked towards Leann hoping she would clearly indicate her agreement with me and looking for as much support as I could garner. "Tony, it isn't going to happen, at least not while you are in our house. So here is our position and our proposition to you. This comes after hours of consideration; I want you to know that. If you decide to drop out of school, you will not be able to live in this home. If you decide right here and now that your choice is to drop out of school, you can take that backpack you walked in with tonight, go upstairs, take some clothes and leave."

As I was saying this, I couldn't believe the words were coming out of my mouth. *Jesus Christ, what am I doing?*

"Your decision to leave school is also a decision that you make knowing you will be on your own….and completely on your own."

Tony looked despondent and confused. I am guessing it looked to him as though he had been surrounded and attacked. Maybe this was the last stand, so to speak. He said nothing. Not a word. No questions. No comments. No anger. He had a blank stare on his face. God, it hurt to see him sitting there. He had no defense. This must have been the worst moment of his young life.

I learned some time ago from author Brendon Burchard that "only two things change your life. Either something new comes into your life, or something new comes from within." I am, however, not convinced it is one or the other.

In my business, I work diligently with agents to bring something new into their life each day, hoping to open their eyes to endless opportunities, which the real estate business surely provides for every single agent. I have also experienced that once I introduce something new into their lives, there are those few (very few) who discover something new, from within, that lights the fire.

I guess I could change Brendon's quote to put into my own words. "I find two things have the power to change your life. First, is the power in grabbing hold of something new that comes into your life; and secondly, finding the ability to grab what is inside of you already, and from within, and combining what is new with what was already inside of you to power yourself forward."

I desperately hoped the solution I had come up with would help Tony do just that.

"So, Tony," I said. This is what is going to happen. You are going to finish out the remainder of the school year to the best of your ability. You will be required to keep a curfew and you will respect all of us. I am not asking, Tony. I am telling you this is what will happen beginning right now. Do you understand?"

He looked up at me and with a nod of his head indicated in the affirmative.

"Tony, should you choose otherwise, you need to make plans to move out of our home. If you intend to fail, we won't support that choice and we will choose not to be part of it. You will not fail on my watch. Next week we will be making application for you to attend a school and program called the Oregon Youth ChalleNGe Program. If you are accepted, and I fully expect that you will be, you will begin the program on July 19th, my birthday. The Oregon Youth ChalleNGe Program is held in a closed facility about 8 miles east of Bend. So, here is what happens at 'The ChalleNGe'...."

As I began to tell him what the program entailed, he bent forward on the couch where he was seated, placed his elbows on his knees, placed his face in his hands and began to repeat over and over ...." Oh no…Oh no…Oh no!"

That moment is forever seared in my memory.

"Tony, you must do this," I stated forcefully. "This is a five and one-half month program where you will be surrounded by other young men and women who have dropped out of school, made serious mistakes, and are looking to recover credits in a supportive and disciplined atmosphere.

"You will have no phone, no television, and no music. There will be times when you will not be allowed to talk. The program is a strict military model where you will address your superiors with "Yes Sir" and "Yes Ma'am" at all times. You will be required to go to bed and to wake at specific times and you will be allowed to visit home three times during this almost 6-month program. We will not be able to visit or speak to you with the exception of the pre-scheduled times. Upon your successful completion of the program, you will be able to obtain 8 high school credits and graduate from the ChalleNGe in December just before Christmas. We will be allowed to communicate by letters only."

He removed his hands from his face and looked up while I was speaking only long enough to get air and compose himself.

"And Tony," I said, my throat closing tighter and with a voice shaking like that of an old man, "I give you my word that I will write to you every day while you are away."

Tears were flowing quite openly from all of us.

"You have to do this, Tony, you just have to," Leann said. She assured him that we wanted this for him because we loved him and we saw it as his last opportunity, his last chance, to graduate successfully from high school.

Introduction

Christiano, sitting next to Nicole, cried, but said nothing at all.

"The deal is, Tony," I continued, "we cannot force you to make application and attend this program. They will only consider candidates who wish to be part of the program. So, you must agree to go. You know you need to go, Tony. You know that your agreeing will be a courageous decision, Tony. Be courageous tonight. Embrace this opportunity. Finally make a decision to change your life. You are worth it, Tony. While you may not realize it right now, this is a gift that will change your life forever."

Tony leaned back with tears flowing freely and blowing his nose repeatedly.

"I know. I understand, dad," he said, the words strained and coming between breaths. "I will do it!"

A feeling of relief came over me, his mother, Nicole, and Christiano.

I reached for a pamphlet I had obtained from the ChalleNGe the day I visited the facility and had spoken to Ms. Rawnsley, an administrator there. Tony looked at it, constantly wiping his eyes and nose. I looked towards Christiano and suggested that he had better get to bed for he had a full day of school beginning in just a few hours. He got up, walked over to Tony, put his arms around Tony's neck and said, "I love you Tony." Tony hugged back and said, "I love you too Yanno."

We were now at that moment that I talked about earlier. First, would Tony grab hold of something new that was about to come into his life, the gift, so to speak; and secondly, would he find the ability to grab what was already inside of him, to power himself forward? This moment indicated a glimmer of hope and a promise of a new beginning. We had needed that ever since things began going south two years before at a football game during his sophomore year.

1

THE BEGINNING OF THE END: SOPHOMORE STRUGGLES

Life presents you with so many decisions. A lot of times, they're right in front of your face and they're really difficult, but we must make them.

Brittany Murphy

You have to always continue to strive no matter how hard things get, no matter how troubled you feel. No matter how tough things get, no matter how many times you lose, you keep trying to win.

LL Cool J

GOING BACK: SEPTEMBER 22, 2005

We settled into our seats on this late Thursday afternoon having driven three hours over the mountain during which we had talked about little else than Tony's upcoming football game, Christiano and me. Three hours over the mountain roads may seem a little much just to watch a JV football game, but that's the kind of family we are. Leann and Nici would have been along for the drive, but neither could leave their work early on this brisk fall day. Driving anywhere to support our kids was a part of who we are. I scanned the field as the pre-game activities were in full swing. No sign of Tony. Everyone else on the team was out there. Where was he? I finally spied the bench. What the heck?

Several of the parents glanced at me and reached out to ask if Tony had suffered an injury that required him to sit out the game. I hadn't seen anything in the pre-game warm-up to indicate that he had suffered any kind of injury, so I just answered them saying, "I have no idea." As the game continued in the first quarter, Tony remained on the bench. Sitting there. Saying nothing. All alone.

Finally, I gained his attention and mouthed the words, "what is going on?" He looked a bit upset and shrugged his shoulders. The longer I sat, the more I questioned what possibilities landed him on the bench sitting alone and not interacting with his teammates on the sidelines.

The waiting was too much, I headed to where Tony was sitting. I had never been the "overbearing father" that stalked the sidelines and interfered with the task at hand for the players and coaches, but this was different.

"Tony," I asked, "are you injured?"

He looked up at me and said, "No dad, the coaches were upset with me and told me to sit on the bench for the remainder of the game."

"Why?" I inquired.

"I don't know dad. I guess I made the coaches mad."

I made my way back to the bleachers. Every parent had watched my every move and every one of them within 10 feet of where I was sitting wanted to know the scoop. I don't know, maybe they had a pretty good idea already, but I told them I had no idea and like Tony, I shrugged my shoulders.

The first half came to a close and each team disappeared into their respective locker rooms. Tony ran off the field with his team without any indication of an injury. No limp, no crutches, and no bandages or ice packs. Parents who had been sitting beyond a general conversation distance to ask about Tony were now headed for the concession stand or bathrooms. Several stopped to ask, "What's going on, why isn't Tony playing?" "Is Tony injured?" "Is Tony ill?"

I didn't have an answer for any of them; but that gut feeling that parents have, you know, the one where you just know? I knew. Deep down in my gut, I knew that it couldn't be good.

Finally, the teams returned from their locker rooms for the second half. As our team ran over to the sidelines, I noticed Tony wasn't in uniform. I looked and I searched for his number #31. No Tony.

Then, I saw him walk over to the bleacher area on the south end of the football field where a few of his friends were sitting. I could see him smiling and joking with some friends and then he walked to the top of the metal bleachers and sat down. He continued to laugh and gist with his friends. I watched in complete dismay. I sat for a minute wondering what was going on and I could see the other parents looking in that direction as well.

Let's face it, alright? I was certain the football parents were aware, from conversations with their kids, that Tony was having issues with his academics at school. That stuff never goes unknown in a small community like ours. I was aware that "everyone" would know about this on Friday. Parents, teachers, friends, and anyone else at the game.

It was now apparent that, not only did he not return in uniform, but that he had taken a seat with some of his rambunctious buddies in the far-end zone bleachers. Needless to say, I was appalled, embarrassed, and as angry as I can ever remember. I asked Christiano to pick up his things. He looked at me with questioning eyes, gathered his belongings, and we walked behind our-team's sideline and towards the exit, which by the way, required us to walk right behind Tony and his group of buddies.

Tony didn't see Christiano and me as we made our way in that direction. He was far too busy yukking it up and enjoying the bleachers. I came to him from behind and asked, quite firmly, "Can you tell me what the hell is going on?"

My presence took him by surprise a bit, but without any delay he said, "Dad, the coaches are just assholes. They told me to sit down away from the team and at halftime they told me to get out of uniform and sit in the bleachers."

At that moment, I was so angry that I could have easily pulled him off the top bleacher and thrown him to the ground for the attitude and disrespect he demonstrated to me. While I spanked my children, there was never a time where any illogical and acceptable punishment might get out of hand. I walked away.

The drive home seemed much longer than the drive to the game. I was too angry to talk. Christiano kept mostly quiet knowing better, or safer at least, than to talk to me. He knew where my mind was, the disappointment I was feeling. Kids are smarter than we give them credit for.

Tony arrived home later that evening on the team bus. He knew better than to call and ask me for a ride home from school. When he walked into the house he acted as if nothing out of the ordinary had happened, dropped his back pack inside the front door and headed upstairs to his bedroom. Before he made his way up the stairs, I asked him to give me one minute of his time. It would take no longer than that for me to say what I wanted to say. I had plenty of time to gather my thoughts on the drive home.

"Tony," I said. I promise you that I will never attend another football game of yours unless you can give me a legitimate reason why you were benched and asked to remove your uniform and apologize to Christiano and me for your actions."

The Beginning of The End: Sophomore Struggles

He just said, "dad, it is nothing I want to talk about."

That's it! He then turned and walked upstairs. He said nothing else. I said nothing else. I left it at that. I didn't approach his coaches. I didn't try to question him any further. And that was the last football game that I ever attended. It broke my heart. I knew I would never watch him play again.

His sophomore football season lasted for 6 more weeks. Not another word about football was spoken in our house. I didn't ask. He didn't offer up anything. The saddest moment came after the season had ended and after having attended his sophomore awards banquet. I did not attend and, in fact, I don't remember that I was aware of this end of season event. He came home, and without a word, left a piece of paper on the kitchen counter; you know, the kind of catch all area for mail, bills, and general put-aside items.

After he went to bed I walked past the counter and noticed the paper. The paper was a special certificate. Tony had been named "The Most Inspirational Player" for the football season. My heart sank. My son, the most inspirational? And I wasn't there to watch him? I wasn't there to share in this one thing, this special one thing where he excelled enough for his teammates and coaches to give him this award. To this day, I have no words to express the sadness for not having found another solution for my anger with his actions. I will never get those moments, those tiny, precious moments back. Until recently we have never spoken of that football season.

* * *

His sophomore year revealed what I believe to be the compounding of not clearly understanding basic foundational concepts that are necessary to continue having the ability to embrace new and more difficult concepts in school. In other words, he was failing and falling quickly.

School had never been easy for Tony. While in the fourth-grade, Tony's teachers, his mother, and I began taking notice of his inability to focus. We saw his inability to read with a normal comprehension level, his challenges with understanding math, and even an inability to focus on the sports field; but then again, he was a 10-year old rambunctious little boy with a splash of piss and vinegar, yet always with a desire to please.

Our concerns and those of his teachers were realized when we received the results from a psychological evaluation conducted at the Pediatric Attention & Learning Disorders Clinic at the University of Iowa Hospitals in Iowa City, Iowa. Leann and I spent the day at the clinic while Tony underwent a complete psychological evaluation by Dr. Lynn Richman, Ph.D. The results of the evaluation and diagnoses revealed multiple concerns: Attention Deficit Hyperactivity Disorder (ADHD), Mild Developmental Reading Disorder, Arithmetic Disorder, and Motor Coordination Disorder. We were stunned.

The testing exposed below average outcomes in associative language, expressive language, memory, academic achievement, and most troubling to me: his attention and impulsivity skills. Our fears were confirmed in Iowa City and left Leann and me so disappointed, as any parent would be.

As he continued to advance from grade to grade, we were constantly reminded by his teachers that he was a polite and kind young man, but that he was often disruptive in class and he was struggling with the work placed in front of him. The impulsivity reared its ugly head on a regular basis, but Tony managed to maintain mostly average grades. Sometimes he achieved above average grades. His social skills and ability to play and participate with friends showed no problems at all. In fact, Tony had a great circle of friends of all academic skill levels.

Tony would often act out without thinking or considering the results of his actions. Thankfully, throughout grade school, middle and high school, Tony stayed out of trouble and showed no indication he was using drugs and alcohol.

The Beginning of The End: Sophomore Struggles

Outwardly, he appeared to be the All-American kid; but this All-American kid was struggling.

I faced the very same issues when I was in school, particularly my freshmen and sophomore years in high school. It was at this time in my life where not having a clear understanding of basic concepts hindered my academic growth. *Dammit!* He was exactly where I had been! It was like looking in the mirror.

In his sophomore year, his grades began to spiral downward. By the second semester, he earned his first F, and in just a year, he was free falling and his mother and I had no idea how to stop it.

One late afternoon, while watching him play basketball as a sophomore on a very talented Mountain View High School basketball team, that the diagnosis given to us six years prior, seemed to secure its credibility. Tony was taller than many of his friends as a sophomore, about 6'3" tall, perfect for a power forward in the MVHS program. He could jump like a deer. Often parents in the stands would turn around and look at us with big smiles when he would soar to the backboard for a rebound. It was almost like they were thinking, "where did that kid come from?" or "did you leave his cape at home?" Sometimes I wondered myself. It was so enjoyable watching him play. I loved every minute of it. It was in this game that I noticed he was having difficulty with visual-spatial and motor integration. It was simple, really.

Without being basketball savvy and without talking the X's and O's of a coach's chalkboard, I could realize that he was unable to see the court and anticipate where the ball needed to be tossed in order to connect with a teammate who was in a position to score. Certainly, there are many moving parts in the game, but his reactions seemed mentally slow and challenged. I suppose I never noticed it before, but in this game, it appeared to me as clear as day that he wasn't able to connect the dots, track the destination of the ball, or anticipate the results of his movements like the other players. *My God. Will*

Tony face even more challenges outside the classroom just playing ball with his closest friends and on his ball team?

I attended all of Tony's basketball games. I don't recall missing more than a couple of all of his sporting events as a child and certainly not in high school. Attending his events were always a priority, like it had been with his sister before him. Leann and I have always placed our children's needs before ours. Nothing spectacular, mind you, we just made it a point to attend anything and everything that our children participated in, whether school plays, swimming, dance, music concerts, parent-teacher conferences, or sporting events.

However, the biggest disappointment came in a Thursday late afternoon JV basketball game a shortly after I noticed the challenge to what I thought might be his spatial and motor skills problem.

I arrived a few minutes late to Tony's Thursday afternoon basketball game. On this day, I had some challenging issues with my real estate work and addressing the needs of one of my 14 agents in my real estate office. When I walked into the gym, I could see that most of the home-team seats were taken and the game was already several minutes into the second quarter. I hate being late to any event, but especially when my kids are involved in whatever activity is taking place. I looked at the scoreboard and stood against the north wall. I remember the score. I don't know why. I don't remember who the opponent was, but I remember the score. It was 19-12. We were in the lead.

I looked at each of the players on the floor and I noted that Tony was not in the game. I looked over to the bench and there was no sign of Tony there either. I thought perhaps he was in the locker room with a sprained ankle and being tended to by the trainer. Tony always seemed to be turning an ankle, for whatever reason. Then I saw the trainer on the bench with the rest of the team and the coaches. *So, where*

The Beginning of The End: Sophomore Struggles

is he? I didn't move. I remained standing against the wall, wondering...

A few minutes later, while the game was in progress, the head coach, Mr. Pinson stood up, made eye contact with me and had an almost woeful look on his face. He looked out on the court and then back at me. It was just a few seconds later that he began to walk my way along the sidelines, all the way across the court to where I was standing. I greeted him with a solid handshake and a very uncomfortable smile, I'm sure. He returned my firm handshake with one, you might say, that appeared uncomfortable and weak.

As we shook hands I greeted him, "Afternoon coach, sorry I missed the first quarter."

He looked at me with bewilderment and asked, "Jim, Tony didn't tell you, did he?"

"Tell me what, coach? I answered back.

"Jim, Tony was dismissed from the team."

My heart sank to the floor with as much force as the basketballs being dribbled by the players. "Why?" I probed.

"Jim, we should probably talk about this after the game, but Tony is not in uniform this afternoon and is no longer on the team. The coaches made a very difficult decision yesterday Jim," he explained.

I'm sure my eyes conveyed the grave disappointment and anxiety I was feeling. I said, "Coach, you better get back to your team. Can I call you later this evening and schedule a time to speak to you?"

He responded, "Of course, Jim, I would also like to schedule a time when head Coach Reid, Athletic Director Dave Hood, and our trainer can be in our meeting."

"Seriously?" I questioned.

"Yes, Jim," he said. "Listen, I need to get back to the team, but just so you are aware, Tony was caught changing a grade on his weekly teacher probation report. He changed a grade that he knew would place him in a position to be eligible to play," he revealed.

"I'm so sorry coach. May I call you around 8 o'clock or so, coach?" I asked.

"Sure, I will wait for your call," he concluded.

We shook hands and he departed.

As Coach Pinson was speaking to me, I could sense that all eyes in the gymnasium were watching me, just as they were at the football game the year before! I mean, think about it. How often have you seen a head coach walk across the gymnasium in the middle of an intense game and engage in a conversation with someone leaning against the wall at the opposite end of the court in a three-piece suit, covered by a trench style black double-breasted X-Long Jaqueta Masculina wool overcoat, and skin tight black Italian leather gloves? I am guessing every parent with a son on the team already knew what I had no idea about. Good lord, if that wasn't a kick in the gut.

I'm sure they were looking at me wondering how they might feel if put in the same position. Perhaps their stares were born out of a sick curiosity, waiting to see what my reaction would be when I found out from Coach Pinson that Tony had been expelled from the team. Maybe their stares were full of pity and sadness. I mean, everyone seemed to love Tony. Were they expecting that I display anger? Might I engage in a shouting match? Or would I break into tears? Frankly, all of them were options vying for top billing in my mind as Coach Pinson relayed the news. My Italian temper has been known to get the best of me from time to time, but not this time; perhaps, because I was in shock.

I have often wondered what was said in the stands by the parents of Tony's friends and teammates. I never discussed this with any of the parents and this to my recollection, was the last time I attended a sporting event at Mountain View High School until my youngest son, Christiano, six years his junior, played sports at the school.

I kept my emotions in check until I reached my car near the exit of the school parking lot. I cried, alone in my car, hoping no one would see me. Every one of us has experienced one of those days when everything seems to go wrong; but, this? How could he do this to me? How could he do this to his family? Where had I gone wrong?

Leann was still at work and Christiano was upstairs in his room when I arrived home just a few minutes after leaving the school and speaking with Coach Pinson. *So now what do we do?* Tony was performing terribly in school, I knew that. The one thing he did well was now gone. No longer would he be part of a team made up of his closest friends with whom he had played ball for years as middle school and high school athletes. Let's be honest, he wasn't going to be a part of the National Honor Society, Young Scholars, or the Advanced Math Club. Was this it?

While I was home alone, sitting in my green chair, I was angry about the way I found out of his dismissal from the team! *Seriously? In front of all the parents, students, team members, and spectators? This is how I find out he was kicked off the team? Dammit! What the hell is wrong with this kid?* As angry as I was, I gave thought to what must have gone through his mind when he found out about his grades? Another failure? The one thing he loves taken away? No longer being part of the team? Or maybe he was scared that he would be in for a serious session of "what the hell is wrong with you" conversation at home? The embarrassment. The disappointment. The despair.

Leann arrived home from work first. "What on earth happened, Jim?" she asked.

I then told her everything that Coach Pinson had told me. She said nothing. What could be said? She marched upstairs, perhaps a little heavier on her feet than normal, to change her clothes.

When she returned downstairs, she sat next to me, and exhaled, "so now what do we do?"

"I don't have any idea, Leann," I replied back.

Minutes later Tony came walking into the house. He walked in looking like nothing had happened, as if it was just another day; but of course, he knew.

My blood pressure rose and my disposition darkened. Certainly, not one of my best moments. I never missed a basketball game, so he knew I wouldn't have missed this one, the one where he was absent. Both Leann and I were still sitting in the living room together.

"Tony, I just came from your basketball game. Would you please sit down and tell your mother and me what the hell is going on with you?"

"I'm sorry, dad," he said with a soft withdrawn voice.

As he found a place to sit and before he could utter another word I began to bark at him. "How could you do this to me? Do you know how embarrassed we are? Why would you have done something like this to me? Mazziotti's aren't cheaters. Everyone in the gym, but me, knew that you had been kicked off the team. I am so embarrassed! Don't you think you might have called and told your mother and me?

He sat there, tears in his eyes, rejected, and taking it all in, showing no anger towards my direct and angry comments. Leann listened to it all. She knew she couldn't add anything between my steady rant; what good would it do anyhow?

At some point, perhaps in a moment when I had to shut up and pause to breathe, he calmly and tearfully said, "Dad, I didn't know what else to do. I failed a quiz on Tuesday. When I made, the rounds getting teachers updates on my grades, I saw that my teacher had placed an F on the report. I knew that would disqualify me from playing on the team. I just couldn't let it happen! I tried not to fail, dad. I really tried," his voice choked with despair.

The Beginning of The End: Sophomore Struggles

"So, Tony, you changed your grade? You actually changed your grade? What were you thinking?" I was fuming.

"Dad, don't you get it!" he said loudly. "I knew this was it! I knew I was done! The only thing I could think to do to stay on the team was to change my grade. I thought maybe I could hand in some extra credit work or something." Then he exploded, "I don't know! I just don't know what to do!"

The room became void of conversation. I had nothing more to say. "Tony, just go up to your room, will you?" I pleaded. He did, leaving Leann and me sitting. There are no words to express how I felt.

Later that evening I called Coach Pinson. The conversation was brief. We scheduled an appointment for the following day to speak with him, the head varsity coach, the athletic director, and the athletic trainer.

* * *

We arrived at the school office about 5:30 to meet with Coach Pinson and the others. I hadn't said much to Tony after our arduous discussion the night before, but I did ask him to tell the truth, to be respectful, and to speak clearly and openly. As Leann, Tony, and I entered the room we were greeted by everyone very professionally. Handshakes were exchanged and the coach was clearly awkward in his movements and mannerisms. He, too, was nervous; clearly, this was not one of his favorite duties as a coach. The athletic director's room looked more like a lounge than an office. I sat with Leann on a couch, which appeared to have been brought in after being discarded from someone's house for new furniture, and Tony sat on a chair across from us and on the left side of a circle that had been formed by the staff. Athletic Director Dave Hood opened up the dialogue welcoming us to "this very unfortunate meeting." Coaches Reid and Pinson reviewed Tony's actions and told us that they were very sorry, but Tony's decision would mean disqualification from the team for the remainder of the season.

It is what I had expected. It now appeared to me that a young boy in his sophomore season would likely not be welcome to join the team in the future. It wasn't exactly said outwardly; but, indirectly the implication was that Tony really didn't need to bother coming back to the team next year or the year after, or any other year for that matter. Don't get me wrong here. The coaches were all doing their best to make a bad situation as tolerable as possible; but I knew, right then and there, that regardless of how Tony might miraculously place himself academically, he would never play another game of basketball on the Mountain View Cougar basketball team. It was as final as final could be. He had played his last game.

His sophomore year ended after being removed from the basketball team and earning a GPA of 1.4615. It couldn't get much worse, could it?

It did.

2
TONY'S JUNIOR-YEAR TAILSPIN

Philosophy is like opening a safe with combination lock: each little adjustment of the dials seems to achieve nothing, only when everything is in place does the door open.

Ludwig Wittgenstein

I believe the school system was completely failing Tony; maybe I was failing him too. A meeting scheduled with the Superintendent of schools, for quite another reason, really brought light to my concern.

It was in June. I had scheduled an appointment with the Superintendent of Schools to present to him an idea that had absolutely nothing to do with Tony or my displeasure with the school district. I scheduled this meeting to propose an idea I had for my real estate business in a cooperative relationship with the school district called Dollars for Classrooms. At this point I was grasping for straws, trying to find business for my struggling real estate office.

My idea was to offer to all teachers, administrators and staff the opportunity for me to give back to the school district an amount equal to 10% of my commission for allowing me the opportunity to list their home or assist in their purchasing a home. I had tried the idea earlier with just one teacher. As a result of my effort the seller and I actually gave back $1000 to the Mountain View basketball team. I thought, why not offer this to the Superintendent as a way to potentially give back to every classroom in our school district that was also fighting through budget issues? The proposal, if presented to district employees, had the potential to gift thousands of dollars back to the classrooms of the school district each year. At the same time the potential for me to finally get my business on track, as a result of this program, was within sight.

Unfortunately, I found that the State of Oregon would not allow for its licensed real estate professionals to engage in a cooperative gifting-back program like the one I had worked so hard to develop. Upon discovery of Oregon real estate law issues and a discussion with the Oregon Real Estate Agency attorneys, I stopped moving forward with the program. It was a staggering blow to many weeks of carefully crafting a business model that, by my very conservative estimate, would generate 100 sales in its first year, at a minimum. In my marketplace one hundred sales at that time would have forwarded $50,000 direct dollars back to classrooms in the Bend-Lapine School District in it's very first year.

Superintendent Nelson was a friendly and approachable administrator. As I proposed my Dollars for Classrooms idea, he leaned forward, clearly listening, and asked all the right questions. The presentation went very well.

As I completed my presentation and was about to leave he asked, "Jim, do you have any children in the school district?"

I answered affirmatively and told him I had two children attending school, one at Buckingham Elementary and another at Mountain View High School.

"So, tell me, you said that you came here from Iowa. How are we doing?"

"In what way, sir?" I inquired.

"Well, are you happy with our school district and do you have any thoughts on how we might improve and be even better?"

At that moment, I was at a loss for words. While my youngest was having a mostly great experience in school, I thought, does he really want to know? "Sir, do you really want my thoughts?"

He answered with a very open and enthusiastic, "Absolutely!"

Over the next twenty minutes I told him, very respectfully, how I thought the school district was failing Tony, and likely other students as well.

I was calm and collected, but I knew my frustration showed. I told him that I had asked for testing for Tony to better understand what might be contributing to his numerous failings and that I had been promised by his high school counselors and administration that they would schedule the testing, but to no avail. One problem that the counseling staff identified was that the "testing people" would need to come to Bend from Portland (a three-hour drive over the Cascades) and their schedules were tight. Nothing was ever scheduled and no one could answer why!

He appeared outwardly concerned, but was very calm and professional. He said, "Jim, there is no reason that I can see for your son not receiving the help he needs and his problems addressed as promised." He asked me for the name of Tony's counselor and he assured me the required tests would be forthcoming. That was the last time I heard from the Superintendent or anyone regarding testing.

I identified the one teacher at Tony's high school who exhibited the ability to build trust and who truly cared about him. A cheerleader, if you will. Joe Padilla taught a Natural Resources biology class to 9th grade students. Tony trusted him because he knew Joe cared. Joe had that "connection" with students; that one teacher with whom a student could connect, talk to; that one teacher with whom a student could say anything to. Some schools have more than a few teachers like that, but at Mountain View High School that seemed to be the exception rather than the rule, at least for Tony.

Several months later, the school year began and we all hoped and prayed that by some act of God things would improve. In October of Tony's junior year, we received his first set of grades. He had received D's in all core classes except for an F in Algebra. Clearly things were spiraling downward. He was in a full tailspin. We tried enrolling him in a very expensive tutoring program at the Sylvan Learning Center for Algebra, but even with some glimpses of progress, the results were mostly the same. While he would come out of a two-hour, one-on-one tutoring session with a math specialist, he just didn't have the basic concepts to build upon and he couldn't acquire new ones without that basic ability! He would walk out of tutoring with a smile and feeling a sense of accomplishment, but he just wasn't able to apply what he had learned at school with any consistency.

Admittedly, after having years to examine my parental duties with acting as Tony's #1 advocate, I should have never allowed the scheduling of many of the classes he was taking. My excuse could easily be that I presumed his school counselor would work closely with him to make sure he was taking classes of value, suitable for his aptitude, and from the required curriculum to graduate; but I knew better. I mean, many of his teachers and counselors had continually failed him for years and I had no indication that anything would ever change; and they certainly did not. I should have done a better job. I did not. There is enough blame to go around, most certainly. To this day, I am unsure whether Tony could have taken different coursework, better suited to his learning ability, and still met the minimum requirements required to graduate.

Tony's Junior-Year Tailspin

At the beginning of the year I saw on his schedule that he was enrolled in a Literature and Composition Class. If I had looked closely at the syllabus for the class I would have seen that it wasn't a class appropriate for Tony and he might have been served choosing another course option, if it was available. I knew that independent reading was essential to successfully engage and complete the course. Knowing this should have motivated me to act, but I didn't. I was frozen in my tracks. I'm not certain why. I guess I was fooling myself that somehow, he would be up for the challenge and that the excitement of a new year, a new beginning, would somehow change past failures.

The syllabus was correct. Much of the home assignments and class time were to be spent independently reading and studying. I encouraged Tony every night to read and to complete his homework. We tried assignment books. Some instructors would check his assignment book for accuracy. I asked him every single night how his school day had been and what homework needed to be addressed; but somehow things slipped through the cracks. I can't explain how. It just did.

On one particular day in October of his junior year Tony told me during our nightly homework conversation that he had been removed from his Literature and Composition Class. When I asked what removed meant he said, "Mr. Trent. kicked me out of the class and asked me not to come back."

I asked him, "what could you have possibly done this time to be kicked-out of a class for the remainder of the semester, Tony?"

He replied, "During our independent reading time I was distracted by a newspaper lying on the floor near the back of the room. As I sat there I thought I would just get up, go pick it up, and place it in the trash."

I probed, "So, you were engaged in reading along with all the members of the class, and you decided randomly to just stop reading, get up from your seat, pick up the newspaper, and throw it away?"

"Yes," he replied.

"And for that you were asked to leave the classroom and not return again?"

"Yes," he innocently acknowledged.

This is the same class where Tony would, for whatever reason, pick up and leave, and interestingly enough, was allowed to do so. Often, he would make his way to Mr. Joe Padilla's classroom and Tony would ask if he had any filing or teacher's aide duties to be completed. When I spoke to Joe Padilla about this, he acknowledged that he knew this was happening and happening often.

Joe said to me, "I knew what was going on and that Tony would leave the school grounds if I didn't provide him safe refuge from this class. I knew that if he was in my room that he would be in school and safe in my classroom. I didn't condone his behavior, but allowed it hoping it was a better alternative."

The next morning, I contacted the Dean of Students with whom I had recently spoken. I asked if I could meet with both him and the teacher who removed Tony from his classroom for the remainder of the semester. He obliged and set an appointment time that would include him, the instructor, Leann and me.

Leann and I arrived for the appointment the next morning and immediately were escorted to Mr. Canon's office. He greeted us with his familiar welcoming smile and told us that Mr. Trent would soon join us. As we sat waiting, he explained his version of what had happened according to Mr. Trent.

"Jim, for Tony to be allowed back into the class, you will need to present both Mr. Trent and me with a "good reason why we might consider it," Dean Canon explained.

I negotiate every day in my real estate business and honestly believe I maintain excellent negotiating skills for my clients and agents; but what I was about to experience had nothing to do with negotiating, or common sense, for that matter.

About five minutes into our brief discussion, Mr. Trent entered the room. He was a man, perhaps 57 years old, with a large face and a stoic countenance. I stood, shook his hand politely and professionally, as the introductions took place. He sat across from me, slightly to my right. Dean Canon sat directly across from me. Leann was immediately to my right. The office accommodated us comfortably, but I was warm, actually very warm, perhaps in my nervousness and discontent.

Dean Canon began the meeting and suggested that we try to find an equitable solution for the benefit of all. We began to discuss Tony and his actions, not only on the "day of the newspaper incident," but of Tony's daily annoyance to Mr. Trent. He was rigid and set. As we talked, trying to find a solution that might allow Tony back into the classroom in order to complete the course, it became evident that Mr. Trent came here, not to find a solution, but to make his intentions known that there was no resolution to this matter.

As I realized this meeting was nothing more than an arranged exhibition of power, I became agitated. As I became angry the volume of the conversation escalated, on my part especially. When it was vividly clear that there was no solution for Tony's return, even for a probationary period, I began to question Mr. Trent.

My questioning admittedly veered into more of an interrogation, questioning Mr. Trent's teaching style, his unfair singling out of Tony, and his refusal to consider giving Tony another opportunity to complete his class. He refused. He sat with his arms crossed, his stomach protruding over his belt, and the buttons of his shirt experiencing the pressure of a shirt too small.

In the course of ten minutes a brick wall was built between the two of us. Dean Canon tried to mediate calmly and professionally, perhaps. I wasn't sure. Leann looked at me with discerning eyes and at this point I knew that I had metaphorically hit the that brick wall. I stood and approached Mr. Trent, seated no more than six feet away. At the same time, sensing things were about to go seriously wrong, Dean Canon stood.

I looked into Mr. Trent's eyes with my finger pointed near, but not touching, his chest, and exclaimed, "Listen, You insignificant piece of shit! Your decision to not give consideration to a workable solution for my son pisses me off! This just isn't right!"

Dean Canon asked me to calm down. I couldn't and I wouldn't.

Abraham Maslow, a famous American psychologist once said, "I suppose it is tempting, if the only tool you have is a hammer, to treat everything as if it were a nail." I had a hammer at that moment. I knew I had to control myself. There was absolutely no positive philosophy for what had just happened. No philosophy at all.

It was at this point that Dean Canon raised his voice and sternly asked, "Mr. Mazziotti, am I going to be required to ask you to leave or worse, call security to remove you from the building?"

It was hopeless. It was entirely ridiculous. I retreated and sat down. Upon sitting down, Dean Canon thanked me and asked if there was any final comment I would like to make before adjourning our little get-together.

I said, "Dean Canon, my wife and I came here looking for a solution that would allow Tony the opportunity to meet the requirements of Mr. Trent's. class." I then looked directly at Mr. Trent and said, "It is evident that no such solution was ever part of Mr. Trent's agenda. Thank you for your time today." I stood, shook the hand of Dean Canon, and walked intentionally away from Mr. Trent as both Leann and I left the meeting quietly.

Our car was parked in the front parking lot of the school, perhaps 30 yards from the front door. Not one word was spoken between us. We were at a loss for words. In the car, we just looked at one another with the same look of disappointment, despair, and anger. I said to Leann, "I don't have any idea what to do. I don't know where to turn and I don't know what to do." There was no slight adjustment to the dials to "open this safe" for Tony. There was no way to open the door.

3
TONY'S SHORT-LIVED ALTERNATIVE SUCCESS

> *To master the discipline of problem-solving you need to develop a formula or method that enables you to deal effectively with almost any problem you face in the course of your career or personal life.*
>
> Brian Tracy

Tony's grades had plummeted from a 1.84 GPA as a freshman to a 1.46 GPA as a sophomore and to a 1.28 GPA as a junior. He didn't have much further to fall! His stable friend base, consisting primarily of athletes he had grown up with playing football and basketball had mostly gone their own direction. Now, his place in the classroom had disappeared, too.

Tony wasn't the only one in trouble. My business bank account, which had been funded by Leann and me cashing in our insurance policies and savings accounts, selling our investment properties in Iowa, borrowing twenty-thousand dollars from my elder brother, and scalping literally every last penny we had, was also disappearing.

Tony's Short-Lived Alternative Success

Bend, had reached new heights in the real estate market, both locally and nationally. In 2006, and now in 2007, the market was in steep decline. Property values were plummeting daily and many who had enjoyed the ecstasy of rising home values and incredible growth were now watching as homes in their neighborhoods were falling into foreclosure.

Leann and I had purchased our home in 2004 and in 2006 took advantage of the opportunity to refinance our home at an extraordinarily low interest rate and interest-only loan and we took the cash from a home equity loan to help fund the opening of my office! It couldn't have been any easier! But now, just one year later, I could see I was facing some huge challenges ahead with my business and, of course, with Tony!

So, the stars were aligned, and not in a good way. I remember thinking about my World History class in 10th grade when my instructor, Paul Frank, had spoken of Germany's two-front war plan in WWII. In that war, Hitler's plan was to conquer Russia on one front and all of Western Europe on another. I remember thinking that I was now well into a "two-front war" of my own. While mine didn't have world significance, but in *my* family's world, it was tremendously significant. On one front, I was fighting to stay in business and on the other front I was trying to save Tony from his freefall.

* * *

The weekend after meeting with Dean Canon and the infamous Mr. Trent. I went to my bookshelf to try and find something I could use to help Tony. In one of my books I discovered a piece of paper hidden within the pages. It wasn't the book itself. It was a piece of paper found inside its cover. I had at one time, maybe from a class I had taken or a lecture I had attended, written down "9 Steps to Solving Problems." However, this one piece of paper included only the first five steps! I am guessing the remaining steps were written on another piece of paper that either had fallen out of the book or had never found its place there. I went to the internet and found Brian Tracy's "Nine-Step Method for Solving Problems Effectively" (from his book *No Excuses: The Power of Self-Discipline*). That was it!

1. Take the time to define the problem clearly.
2. Ask yourself, "Is it really a problem."
3. Ask, "What else is the problem?"
4. Ask, "How did the problem occur?"
5. Ask, "What are all the possible solutions?"
6. Ask, "What is the best solution at this time?"
7. Make a decision!
8. Assign responsibility.
9. Set a MEASURE for the decision!

I used these steps to create a plan for Tony. It looked like this:

Tony Mazziotti's 9 Step Program to Success

1. What is the problem with Tony?
Tony clearly suffers from ADHD. His lack of ability to focus and his inability to not act, at times *impulsively*, have now placed him in a position of being unable to successfully complete high school. He wants to quit. There is no way we can allow him to become a high school drop-out. The Bend-Lapine School District has failed Tony. Perhaps I have failed him too. We need to find a school where he can find success and graduate.

2. Is it really a Problem?

Yes. He is unhappy. He has lost his friend base of kids, those with whom he primarily played sports from 8th to 11th grades. He is currently associating with kids whom I don't believe can "raise him up," but rather "bring him down." The school district has failed and there is no indication that promises they made will ever be kept. I, too, am not without blame. But now is the time to act.

3. What else is the problem?

I believe he has a supportive family and home. I do not see any problems other than a low self-esteem, and if he drops out of school, he will likely fail in life.

4. How Did The Problem Occur?

The problem has been compounded due to his inability to establish strong foundational pieces in his education. Now "the compounding effect" has left him with the inability to "fake it until you make it." His inability to focus and his clear impulsiveness has left him making bad decisions that in time will only lead him to more destructive decisions.

5. What Are the Possible Solutions?

With the cooperation of Dean of Students, Mr. Mike Cannon, transfer him into an alternative school called COIC, which is a school that will allow him to earn credits both in the classroom and in an outdoor work program. I think this will appeal to him. Our hope is he can complete his high school diploma requirements.

6. What Is the Best Solution at This Time?
COIC (#5)

7. Make A decision!
Done. Leann and I will contact Mr. Canon to transfer him immediately.

8. Assign responsibility
Me!

9. Set A measure for the decision
The measure has been set and the measure is placing him in the school first. Next, it is up to me to make absolutely certain he is completing all assignments, attending all classes, and meeting every guideline to graduate. It is about me!

* * *

I have read the words of John Maxwell, who suggests that *attitude* is all about eliminating negative words and adopting positive words. He suggests removing these words and short phrases from your vocabulary: I can't. If only. I don't think. I don't have time. Maybe. I'm afraid. I don't believe.

Instead, he suggests using: I can. I will. I know. I will make the time. Absolutely. I'm confident. I'm sure.

Great suggestion, but *really*! Tell that to a kid who is facing a constant uphill battle in school, whose abilities or inabilities (as it may be) are challenged every day by all those around him, and now who has been kicked off the basketball team.

John Maxwell is correct in suggesting that continually looking for and embracing the positive in order to eliminate the negative will help us begin thinking more positively every day; but, I am sure he didn't have my son in mind when recommending this theory. I wish I had considered taking the "positive attitude" approach with Tony earlier. Not only the night when I found out Tony had changed his grade to remain eligible to play basketball, but always.

Maybe my mistake will help you in thinking about positive words. I know that in my real estate business I grasp for positive words to inspire and motivate my agents; so, why wouldn't I consider this the correct way to deal with family matters?

* * *

*Sometimes the darkest challenges, the most difficult
lessons, hold the greatest gems of light.
Barbara Marciniak, author*

I don't know whether I had ever seen Tony happier with a school program than he was with COIC. He would go to school each morning with a brown lunch bag, blue jeans, and work boots, perhaps more commonly worn by construction workers. He spent half his school days working on natural resources projects by creating and restoring trails, walkways, hiking bridges, and even some campsite restoration in the Deschutes National Forest along gorgeous rivers and abundant wildlife. He would return with his work crew and then spend a few hours in the classroom to handle the academic requirements of the program. The instructors were caring and genuine. He worked closely with Chris Stokes, an excellent role model and caring teacher at COIC.

Unfortunately, while Tony appeared to benefit from the structure of the program, he was not particularly happy with his new social scene.

I would take Tony to the school each morning and unlike the campus atmosphere of his traditional school, this school was located in a commercial area in a building that appeared to have been modified from its initial best use as a commercial office space, to a school classroom. Each morning we would pull into this unorthodox school setting and we saw kids hanging out just like many schools throughout America; but this place just didn't feel the same.

Not making new friends at the Alternative School caused Tony to miss his old friends even more. Because he was separated from his friends at MVHS, it became more difficult to socially adjust and to move forward. There are no clubs or sports teams at COIC. You go there for one purpose: to take classes and hope to have the opportunity of being placed in an outdoor work study program.

The kids come and go. I could identify groups of students gathered outside the school's fenced areas. Many of the kids, along with their associates, were having that last cigarette before the start of classes or their first cigarette after school. Most of these kids seemed to be friends. Tony didn't fit their M.O. He just didn't. When I dropped him off on my way to work each morning, he walked straight into the building and when I picked him up at the end of the day he would come directly to our car. I never saw him socializing with the other students and I know he never befriended anyone in his two-month experience at COIC.

He passed all of his classes; but there was something amiss in his attitude.

One day in March everything changed.

4

LOOKING FOR A WAY OUT

*Sometimes we stare so long at a door that is closing
that we see too late the one that is open.*

Alexander Graham Bell

*Tear gas is a good teacher. It taught me that what they say is
true: Awful conditions can bring out the best in people.
It taught me that one can get used to almost anything,
including a sensation of choking, and of impending death.
It taught me to savor the simple pleasure of fresh air.*

Zeynep Tufekci

As Tony's life was quickly dismantling, I looked for anything I could find to help stop the pain of it all. During the past several years, it seemed that there was always some crisis with Tony. I know I'm not the only parent who has ever felt overwhelmed and helpless, but I sure felt alone in that at the time.

Once again, I turned to my bookshelf. Over the years, I have gathered many books on both parenting and business. I was looking for the book, *7 Habits of Highly Effective Teens,* by Sean Covey, which thankfully I had purchased on December 6, 2006. I know this because the receipt was still in the book.

God, please let there be something, anything, here to help Tony.

In the Covey tradition, the book is packed with everything a parent could want to guide their child into becoming the model student and the perfect child; yet, that is if we were in a perfect world. Everything doesn't go as planned; we know that. Surely there would be something from this book that would help stop the bleeding.

Have you ever opened a new book, began to flip through the pages while previewing it, and have it open up to the exact page you needed in that moment? Happens all the time to me. So, I put the book in my hands and did the page flip. I'll never forget the first page that I landed on and what was right in front of my eyes. It was a poem by an unknown author, called "Who Am I?" I read it. Slowly. Line by line.

WHO AM I?

I am your constant companion; I am your greatest helper or heaviest burden.

I will push you onward or drag you down to failure. I am completely at your command.

Half the things you do might just as well turn over to me and I will be able to do them quickly and correctly.

I am easily managed - you must merely be firm with me.

Show me exactly how you want something done and after a few lessons, I will do it automatically.

I am the servant of all great people; and alas, of all failures as well.

Those who are great, I have made great.

Those who are failures, I have made failures.

I am not a machine, though I work with all the precision of a machine plus the intelligence of a human.

You may run me for a profit or run me for ruin - it makes no difference to me.

Take me, train me, be firm with me, And I will place the world at your feet.

Be easy with me, and I will destroy you.

WHO AM I?

I AM HABIT.

Author Unknown

The line "Be easy with me, and I will destroy you," grabbed me by the throat. Almost literally. I laid the book in my lap, with my thumb marking the page. *Be easy with me, and I will destroy you. Is it time?*

I would like to think I developed pretty good work habits in my life. Not all my habits are good, but my work habits, yes. As an Iowa boy, my father taught me well. Those that know me are painfully aware that I am far from perfect; but, they do know I work and I work hard. I guess it became habit.

Tony had succumbed to bad habits and my real estate team seemed to bring the same concerns to the table each day mostly ruled by doing their work the same way Tony approached school: going about life looking for the easy way. The adverse effects of the easy way seemed to be destroying Tony, the agents in my office, and me.

I knew at that moment that to save Tony and myself from being destroyed, I must take action. This would become my mantra, which I would implement as a parent and as the leader of my real estate company.

I decided that it was time to figure out what was going on in Tony's head.

* * *

I picked up the phone and placed a call to Mr. Canon, the Dean of Students at Mountain View High School. I updated him on Tony's progress and we spoke about suggestions he might have to help Tony, perhaps to include re-enrollment at MVHS with his old classmates. As we spoke, and trying my best to convince myself everything was progressing nicely, Mr. Canon sensed my uneasiness.

"Jim," he said, "why don't you schedule a test with one of our local school psychologists?"

I replied, "Well, do you think that would really be beneficial?"

"Jim," he explained, "we don't know what's going on in Tony's head, how he is really feeling about his life, school, friends, and the future. I will send you a name of a guy. Give him a call if you believe it would be beneficial to you and to Tony."

Shortly after the call, I received the name of a school psychologist who has a private practice in Bend. I called the office of Dr. Prignano. (He must be good, after all, he is Italian, right?) We set an appointment to meet just a couple days later. I was pleased how quickly he would be able to speak to us.

Leann and I arrived a few minutes early for our appointment with Dr. John Prignano. His office was located in a quiet, quaint little house that had been converted to serve as his office in the trendy area on Colorado Street in Bend. We pulled up in front and saw a sign asking for clients to walk through the gate, alongside the house and through the back door. His office was simple, in professional office standards, but comfortable. While it was the Christmas season there was no evidence of it in his office. Dr. Prignano had no secretary to receive us. Instead, he rose from his desk, located in a small room close to the door and greeted us warmly. He guided us through the process he uses to work with students to assist them learn to cope more effectively with life issues and mental health problems.

I would like to spend about an hour with you today, Mr. and Mrs. Mazziotti," he said. "My goal is to look at the issues that brought you here today concerning your son, Tony. It is my hope that together we can help both you and your son at Mountain View High School. I will meet with the two of you today and I would like to schedule a time for me to meet with Tony. Then, after I complete my evaluation, I will forward my conclusions directly to Mr. Canon at Mountain View High School, and if necessary, meet with both of you and Tony."

"Sounds, good," I stated. "Where do we start?"

We spent the next ten minutes with both Leann and me giving him Tony's background, providing him with Tony's evaluation performed at the University of Iowa hospitals in 2000, covering issues that have plagued Tony for years, and making sure he understood our family dynamic. I knew that as the primary psychologist for student evaluations at Mountain View High School that he met with many types of kids and many variations of family, some good and some bad, and well, some very bad. So, I wanted him to know a little about our family.

I told Dr. Prignano I believed our family was and is a family built on several foundational pieces that are non-compromising. First, as a family, I believe we are spiritually centered and faith driven. I remember telling him, "Doc, I believe you would find that our family lives knowing that there are absolute moral truths that can't be compromised. Those include the importance of a commitment to faith, the strength of family, and knowing that generosity and valuing growth make us good people and an even better family." At the same time, quite honestly, I was questioning my own spiritual leadership and knowing that the "strength of family" was being tested, really for the first time for Leann and me.

As I look back now, I realize that I had borrowed those same foundational pieces to build my new company. In fact, the same values I told the doctor are the same core values I used for my company: operating with uncompromised ethics; behavior and moral truths; building the strength of a collaborative real estate team; instilling the goal to give back to our community through personal generosity and philanthropy; and working always to grow in reaching our God-given potential.

I told Dr. Prignano how our family took immense pride in our name and our Italian heritage going back at least to Tony's great grandfather, Frank Mazziotti. Frank, upon arriving in a small, northeastern Iowa town at the turn of the twentieth century, worked hard and at the onset of good fortune and an expanded business, began assisting and funding other Italian families to come from his small village in Longobucco, Italy, to Iowa for both jobs and an education. Mark Twain told his audiences, perhaps tongue-in-cheek, that he had spent a large sum of money to trace his family tree and then spent twice as much trying to keep his ancestry secret. Well, that isn't the case with our family.

I recalled Tony, at his most frustrated moment, telling me he wanted to quit school and I recall exclaiming, "Tony, Mazziotti's don't drop out of school. It has never been an option for any Mazziotti, and it certainly isn't an option for you." At the same time, I told him about his great grandfather and the need for him to finish school knowing that without the stability education offers he might never have the option to experience his own significance.

I told Tony, "Your great grandfather and grandfather worked hard to provide you and me with a family name built on significance. If you owe no one else anything, think of them." I know that he knew that our family and our home would always be a safe haven in a storm; but this was the big test for all of us. I know Tony was at his wits end with school and with life in general. He had experienced constant and consistent failure at about every turn. I wouldn't allow for the words "broken" and "dysfunctional" to become part of any sentence with our name in it, and certainly not Tony's.

As we talked with the doctor, we told him of our concerns about Tony: his difficulties in school and especially with math; that the school had come to us in November of 2005 suggesting that perhaps Tony should be considered for special education (which was nothing more, in my opinion, than to pass him off for lost and this further demonstrated how out of touch his counselor was with his needs); that his self-image was damaged; and that he was impulsive and struggling. We told him that the prescription he had been taking (Concerta) for ADHD had little to no effect overall. We spoke of his emotional wellness, or lack of it.

"Do you know whether Tony has ever contemplated suicide?" the doctor asked.

Thankfully, suicide, to our knowledge had never been a consideration. Tony was mostly upbeat, was able to always make friends, and had great social skills. He had never exhibited any outward anger to us or his family, only frustration, as I saw it.

"Is he using alcohol or drugs?" he further inquired.

"The only drugs he's using are those prescribed by his doctor," I told him. "We have seen no evidence of alcohol."

Both of which were true. He asked about any family history of depression, mental illness, alcohol, and drug abuse. Jesus, it is estimated that more than 50 million Americans suffer from some kind of mental disorder in a given year with more than 200 classified forms of mental illness! My opinion is that most of us are a little off our rocker, but I knew that wasn't the answer he was looking for and it wasn't the answer I gave to him.

My mother had suffered from what I recall was a chemical imbalance that showed itself in the form of mild depression, but I also recollect that it was handled quite easily once diagnosed and treated with mild medications. I had a wonderful Uncle, on my mothers' side, who had committed suicide in the late 1960's and who had been suffering from depression most of his adult life. My father's side, our Italian side, does quite frankly, fit some of the stereotypes, many negative, Italians seem to own almost exclusively. If those stereotypes include "overly interested in food," "hot tempered," "talk with their hands," and are "loud and obnoxious," well, let the cards fall where they may. God knows I have family on my fathers' side who fit some or all of these characteristics, including some of which I possess; but I don't recall or know any diagnosed issues with mental problems or alcohol in my immediate family.

Leann wasn't acutely aware of any mental illness on her side of the family. And while her parents enjoyed more than their share of alcohol, there was no official diagnosis of alcoholism, of which she is aware. I know enough about mental illness, alcohol abuse, and drug abuse to know that one or all aren't exclusive to any one trigger, so this issue was beyond that concern.

The doctor asked that we both speak openly, even if that meant that our opinions differed from one another. Both Leann and I were totally forthright with the doctor. She told him that our three children knew there was little "give" in my expectations for them. Each was expected to do their very best and to achieve nothing less than a B average in school. Tony, like his older sister, knew that they would not be allowed to drive or even test for a license unless they met our, or rather, my expectations. As a result, Tony did not get his license until shortly before the age of 19. He knew enough, I guess, to never even ask. There was never even a discussion concerning a license. Leann told the doctor that my expectations were likely understood by Tony as being "on him" all the time.

Perhaps it was. Much was expected of the first Mazziotti boy born to his fraternal grandparents.

As we came to the conclusion of our meeting with Dr. Prignano, we all agreed that based on our interview there didn't appear to be any family issues or other indicators that pointed to any disturbing conclusions. There was an absence of drugs and alcohol, there was no abuse, and we truly loved one another.

"It looks to me like we may have a young man who simply dislikes school," the Doctor pronounced.

We finished our interview with Dr. Prignano in less than an hour. Before leaving, we scheduled an appointment for Tony six days later on December 21, 2006.

Doctor Prignano called me a few days before Christmas to tell me he needed to complete drafting his opinion, but in general he found those things we had identified and little more. "Tony told me that he has dealt with academic difficulties for the past several years, had recently broken up with a girl who had actually tried to commit suicide with a drug overdose herself, that he enjoyed playing video games, that his parents are strict but always there for him, and that he is able to talk best with his older sister. He denied any problems with depression or thoughts of suicide, that he gets anxious easily, and that he has plans after graduation to enlist in the Navy and become a fire fighter after serving four years in the armed forces."

He added, "I guess you could say he is a young man with some learning difficulties, but little more. My notes indicate that Tony is a pleasant, polite, and engaging young man who describes his parents as strict, but knows he is loved."

The doctor had told Tony that he would be happy to visit with him again, if Tony wished, but that no further need for counseling was either necessary or required.

The conversation had long ended. The talk about dropping out of school was addressed. Tony understood that the only way he was likely to have the opportunity to finish high school was to take several steps. We discussed them at length.

Tony had finally come to realize that choices which are easy in the short term are very often smack dab in direct conflict with what makes life easy in the long term. In other words, there was no easy way out.

5
THE DARKEST HOUR

Challenges are what make life interesting and overcoming them is what makes life meaningful.

Joshua J. Marine

I hadn't slept much after another concerning day. Tony's unhappiness with his new school's social scene had begun to undermine his new-found positive academic performance. Meanwhile, more business issues required immediate action on the real estate front. On and on it went.

I woke up about as low as I could remember. I was working on a personal marketing campaign and trying desperately to find new business. My agents weren't producing in numbers to sustain the overhead and commitments of my office. I had told the few agents I had in my office that I would serve as their mentor and trainer and I would not engage in personally working with buyers or sellers in taking the cream of the crop calls and leads coming into our office (a practice which is so widely a part of real estate offices all over America).

My goal was to develop a one-of-a kind company. I spent everything I had in purchasing, what I still believe is the very best real estate franchise in North America, but my personal model was much different than my franchise brand and other franchise companies. Some told me that the "utopian" model I desired would never work. My model was to build a "30-20" office. That is, an office where 30 agents would be invited to be part of the model and my company, with me working diligently to assist each in attaining 20 sales per year, at a minimum, and in a small, comfortable, but non-audacious office, in an atmosphere where they could see that my investment was not just in the bricks and mortar of a structure; instead, my investment would be in them.

I had proposed my company model directly to then USA President for Exit Realty Corporation International, Tami Bonnell, in early 2006. As we sat with regional owner of Exit Realty Oregon, Bruce Caruth, in a beautiful suite on the fourth floor of the Sheraton Hotel in Portland after a wonderful Exit-sponsored event, I expressed to her my vision for my new company. I had interviewed other franchises. Frankly, in my opinion, the franchise sales managers for the other franchise brands had one goal in mind; to sell a franchise regardless of the applicant's needs. Sometimes you can smell it. I had with every other company I had visited.

Tami was different. While her franchise had rules and guidelines, she listened. I knew she was listening while I was speaking from the heart of my vision, if allowed to build it. After 40 minutes, she extended her hand out to me and said she would welcome my company as one of the newest franchises should we be able to consummate the details and paperwork. Now, just months after opening, the wheels were falling off the bus, much like my personal life with Tony and his excruciating challenges that were front and center every single day!

My life was a metaphor for tough circumstances. I was fighting fire with fire. Here in the Northwestern United States we are the victims of many summer forest fires. The fires devastate the landscape and the beauty of the forest, and it costs millions to fight and it requires the resources of thousands of men and women, some of whom give their lives. The concept of fighting fire with fire comes from a technique of putting a barrier between two burning fires until they burn towards each other and when all things go correctly, burn themselves out.

I saw no such resolution to my problems. On one side of the forest succumbing to the flames shooting high in the sky, I had one out of control fire – Tony. On the other side was an equally threatening fire burning hot and burning fast – my business. I was the strip of cleared or plowed land used to stop the spread of the fire or the barrier. But the question was, could I actually get these two fires to burn themselves out? Pauline Phillips, who was also known as the famous newspaper columnist, Dear Abby, once said to one of her readers seeking her advice, "People who fight fire with fire usually end up in ashes." It certainly appeared that her advice to her reader might apply in my life.

I walked into my office shortly after noon. As I walked through the front door, I was greeted with a cheerful welcome from my secretary. Carly had been my secretary as I was putting together my new franchise and well before the doors ever opened. She knew many details of my life and certainly the drama with Tony. In fact, I had asked her to sit with Tony to see if she might be able to help him with his Algebra, which she worked hard to do, but ended up suggesting a professional tutor at our local Sylvan Learning Center, which we did with very little success.

"How is your day, Jim," she asked.

"Awful, Carly," I replied. "Last night was the worst. Last night Tony told Leann and me that he thought he would just quit school and find a job somewhere. I told him that should he decide to quit school he would not be allowed to live with us and he would need to find somewhere else to live."

"What did he say," Carly asked.

"I don't know, something like 'that is so stupid,'" I recalled.

I felt as though I was near that "darkest hour" which I had read in a poem or heard in a song. And I was. So was our entire family. It couldn't have been much better for Tony, now that I reflect on it.

Then the words that would change our lives.

"Jim," Carly said, "you need to look into the Oregon Youth ChalleNGe."

"What is that," I asked?

"It is a school east of Bend. It is a school that is a place for kids who are in trouble or who have dropped out of school. I remember a couple of kids who went there when I was in high school."

"Where is it," I asked.

She reached to the right-hand side of the desk and pulled out the phone book. She grabbed a piece of scratch paper and wrote down 23861 Dodd's Road. I knew where Dodd's Road was. I had shown property out in that direction before.

No sooner had she handed me the address then I was out the door and headed to my car.

"Carly, I am going out there right now. I don't have any appointments this afternoon?"

She acknowledged with a "Nope!"

I was in my car and on my way. I would soon find out that the 17-month ChalleNGe Program was a result of a project undertaken by the Center For Strategic And International Studies in the late 1980's and 1990's. Its goal was to consider and develop new approaches for out-of-school youth in America. Staff in the National Guard Bureau in the U.S. Department of Defense developed the specific program model. They designed the Youth ChalleNGe to be:

> ....an intervention, rather than a remedial program. We would deal with the symptoms and underlying causes in a construct that fully embraced a "whole person" change and readied the students for the post-program

environment. We would arm them with the skills and experiences necessary to succeed and we would ensure there was "a way back" to mainstream society.

In 1993, Congress funded a 10-state pilot of the ChalleNGe Program. Today there are 40 ChalleNGe programs in 28 states, Washington D.C., and Puerto Rico. While most states operate a single 100-bed program while serving about 200 participants per year in two-class cycles, the Oregon Youth ChalleNGe, in which Tony was a cadet, serves up to 320 participants per year.

While each program has the ability to design their individual curriculum to meet local conditions, the basic structure is the same in all states. Open to boys and girls between 16-18, the program was designed for youth who have dropped out of or been expelled from school. They must be unemployed, drug free, and not heavily involved in their state's justice system.

The only thing that makes life possible is permanent, intolerable uncertainty; not knowing what comes next.

Ursula K Le Guin, American Author

The drive was a little over seven miles from my real estate office. In about 12 minutes I had arrived at my destination. As I drove up the long driveway, I passed a check point that was apparently a remnant of the facility's past use. Closer to the building, a parameter had been established with a metal fence, maybe eight feet high with barbed wire at the top; customary for a military installation I guess, but a school?

I looked and identified what I thought might be the front entrance to the facility. The glass door was locked and it required that I enter into a vestibule where I would need to press a buzzer to gain permission for entrance. I had to think for a minute before hitting the buzzer. *Did I really want to hear what I was about to hear?* I pushed the buzzer. It was just a few seconds before I was greeted by a young girl, perhaps 16, her dark hair tied tightly back, in military issue-type clothing and she said, "Good afternoon Sir, how might I help you?" I told her I was hoping to speak with someone who might be able to address some questions I had about the facility and the program.

"Give me just a minute, sir. Have a seat right here." she stated.

About three or four minutes later a middle-aged woman came out into the waiting area and welcomed me. "Good afternoon, sir. How might I help you today?" she inquired. I told her that I had been directed to the facility by my secretary who thought this program might be able to help my son.

She acknowledged my request and said, "Please step into our conference room."

When she opened the door, another meeting was coming to a close and the individuals acknowledging that she required the room, quickly stood, and quietly left.

"My name is Karen Rawnsley, the Deputy Director here at OYCP," she said. "So, Mr. Mazziotti, tell me about your son."

For the next few minutes I explained to her the challenges we had been facing for years with Tony. She had been writing notes on a yellow pad that she grabbed from somewhere in the room before we began the conversation.

"Can you give me one specific example of where you feel he and the school have recently failed to address the problems he is having," she probed.

At that moment, the incident he had with Mr. Trent, his teacher from Mountain View High School, came to mind.

"Yes, I can," I said confidently. "My son, Tony has difficulty being able to focus on numerous tasks. He told me that in one of his classes, where mandatory class time reading is required, sometimes for more than an hour without a break, that he is unable to sit and read for the entire class period.

His teacher finds that the best way to address the issue is to allow him to leave the classroom.

"The teacher *allows* him to leave the classroom?" she questioned.

I replied, "Yes, that is my understanding."

"So where does he go?" she asked.

"Well, I think sometimes he just goes out into the hallway. Sometimes I think he finds his way to another teacher's room where he has served as an aide. Actually, I think the teacher is just glad to have him out of his hair."

At that moment, she asked me to stand. She looked around the room and grabbed a book that had been on one of the shelves.

"Mr. Mazziotti, may I ask you to hold your arms straight out and extended in front of you."

"Okay," I said.

"Now, while keeping your arms fully extended, open this book, hold it in your hands and begin to read to yourself quietly. Let me know when your arms can no longer support the book and when you need to put the book down," she instructed.

I don't remember how long it was, but it wasn't very long at all before fatigue became an issue. My arms were weakening. Now, I'm a big man, so I didn't want to show weakness, but my arms were beginning to shake and before too long I needed to put the book down.

"I'm done. I don't think I can hold the book like that for another second," I stated, wondering why she had just put me through this humbling exercise.

"Mr. Mazziotti, at the Oregon Youth ChalleNGe, we do not allow the students to get up, to leave the room, or to walk aimlessly around our facility. I used this example of your holding the book to emphasize what would be the result of your son NOT following our instructor's directions to read, regardless of the amount of time required. You see, the students at the

ChalleNGe aren't asked to do something lightly. The cadets here learn that should they wish not to follow our guidelines that there will be consequences to their action. In the situation you described, your son would have clearly understood that his not wanting to read would be welcomed with firm action and consequences, much like you just experienced.

"During our 22-week residential phase, your son, if able to meet our admission guidelines and invited to the ChalleNGe, would not have the ability to question authority. We have clearly defined standards that cadets must achieve to successfully be a part of our program. While we are not a military school, we are a military-style school where our cadets are not given the ability to question authority," she explained.

She asked me to follow her to an area that overlooked a large room that one might describe as an interior parking area for a large number of trucks and vehicles. I later learned it was the "drill floor" for the facility. It had a high ceiling and a poured cement concrete floor that looked as if it were clean enough to eat off of. Clearly, attention was given to this floor to perfection. I had noticed a young man near the center of the room on his hands and knees, a puddle of water before him, a pail, and a sponge in his hand.

"Do you see that young man, Mr. Mazziotti?" she asked as she put her hand up to the glass and pointing in his direction.

"That young man has been on our floor for the past hour. He is there because he failed to follow instructions." she explained.

"Our cadets all know that there are consequences for their behavior here at the ChalleNGe. I am guessing that this young man made the wrong choice and I would guess this will be the last time he makes the same choice," she said.

"During my years at the ChalleNGe," she began to say, "I've discovered something from an ancient Chinese proverb, 'A wise man adapts himself to circumstances as water shapes itself to the vessel that contains it.'"

It was clear, as she continued to outline the requirements of both the youth and their parents, that this was about as tough as it gets for kids like Tony. She left me with information on the ChalleNGe, invited me to make application to attend the next orientation, and guided me back to the front door, wishing me much success with Tony.

I remember driving home from my meeting thinking, is this really something that we are going to be required to do? Is there no other option? Could I actually drop my son off here and leave him?

6

ORIENTATION

*Effective prayer is prayer that attains what it seeks.
It is prayer that moves God, effecting its end.*

Charles G. Finney

Tony had answered the question of whether I could leave him at the ChalleNGe program the night he chose, once again, to stay out until the wee hours of the morning. Nothing we had said or done had made a dent. Something had to give.

Giving him the ultimatum to either attend Youth ChalleNGe (go to TheChallengeStory.com for more information about the program) or leave home was about as hard as anything I'd ever done. Until his mother and I took him to the Orientation Day.

I knew that if Tony failed to earn a high school diploma, he was likely to never find success in his life, a *lose-lose* situation. Today was about finding a *win-win*, and the belief that there are second chances and alternatives for him.

The Youth ChalleNGe program, managed by the National Guard Youth Foundation, was designed with three phases. Phase 1 is called the Pre-ChalleNGe. This phase begins when the youth enter the program and it is an intense two-week period. The first two weeks are physically and psychologically demanding! The students are referred to as "candidates" in this first phase. They are introduced to the strict rules and expectations and they learn military bearing, discipline, and teamwork and man, it is strict! People say it's as tough as the first two weeks of boot camp in the Marine Corps! It is in this first two-week period that students who wish to withdraw usually do. Those that stay and complete this program have endured the hardest two weeks of their lives.

Students who complete the Pre-ChalleNGe are formally enrolled in the program as "cadets" and they now move to the next phase of the program. This next phase is known as the "20 Week Residential Phase." Compared to the brutal first two-week period, this next period, according to Tony, is almost like a vacation or a walk in the park. This phase is structured around eight core components:

1. Leadership/Followership
2. Responsible Citizenship
3. Service to Community
4. Life Coping Skills
5. Physical Fitness
6. Health and Hygiene
7. Job Skills
8. Academic Excellence.

It is at this time the new cadets spend the largest part of their day in the classroom.

During the Residential Phase, great care is taken to minimize negative effects of placing "at-risk" cadets together in a program setting. This was something Leann and I were the most concerned with when making application to The Oregon Youth ChalleNGe. While Tony was easily a candidate for dropping out of school, he had no prior evidence of the use or abuse of alcohol or drugs at all. He had no legal issues, no gang activity, and as his mother and I viewed him, Tony was a nice kid who had little interest in completing high school. It was little wonder, actually. The kid was dealing with what I call "compounded academic failure."

* * *

We arrived for the orientation at 7:45 a.m., forty-five minutes before the scheduled start, after which Tony would decide if he was ready to shake the *lose-lose* scenario that had its arms wrapped around him in a strangle-hold.

A few parents were arriving with their kids, both male and female, and finding a place in the parking lot located just north and west of the large building that housed the ChalleNGe, but it was apparent we were early. We usually were. As we walked up to the front door there were two young ladies standing just outside the main entrance dressed in military fatigues. They had been placed there to direct us to the presentation room and greeted us with "Good morning, sir" and "Good morning, ma'am." It is what you might expect walking into a military facility, but not what you would ever find in a normal public high school.

Inside the door several more boys and girls, placed strategically, guided us through several hallways en route to our final destination. The floors were concrete and the walls were painted a light tan color with the metal door frames painted teal. We passed several unoccupied offices where it was apparent someone worked, perhaps on a daily basis. The desks and tables were reflective of perhaps a bygone era. Metal desks, big and clunky chairs, some apparent wear and tear around the door frames, and an overall building showing its age.

Orientation

This was not the Taj Mahal by any means. We learned later that this facility had, at one time, served as a secret military communications installation that had the ability to do vision tracking during the cold war. In fact, it was built to withstand a nuclear blast! Well, at least it would be the safest place for Tony to be if someone happens to push the button.

As we stepped up into the main presentation room, there were two more young cadets, also dressed in fatigues, handing out paperwork and directing us to our chairs.

"Sir," the young cadet said, "please have your son be seated in the first two rows to the front of the room. You and your wife are welcome to take a seat anywhere else you feel comfortable."

Tony, without further instruction, walked to the front and found a seat in the front row. Leann and I sat behind him, so as not to interfere and distract him from the presenter and any instructions intended for the candidates. It was clear that this room was a large classroom. There were some old bookshelves, a couple of desks, and a large screen to the front of the room. I would say the room was 60 x 40, more or less, and there were maybe 125, fold-out metal chairs set up in two sections with an aisle down the middle.

Because we were early we were able to sit comfortably where we could see the parents and candidates walk in. As each candidate walked in with his or her parents, I tried to visualize and guess what might have brought them to this meeting. I later learned that we were in the first group of two separate orientation sessions that would be conducted on this Saturday. Our session would run from 8:30 to 12:30pm. The OYCP has room for only 156 cadets per class, of which there are two classes each year. More than 250 youth apply for the 156 spots and the selection process is precise, strict, and firm guidelines are established.

For this first session there were, I would guess, 50 kids, about half boys and half girls. There were perhaps another 100 parents. Some of the young candidates were accompanied by one parent or even a grandparent, but there was mostly a male and female adult with each young candidate. The kids looked to be between 15-18 years old. The guidelines for entrance require that an accepted candidate to the program cannot have reached the age of 19 on the day of entrance and must be at least 16 on the day of entrance as a minimum. The program does not allow for any negotiation on this matter.

As we sat awaiting the start of the orientation, a cast of characters was making themselves known, either by choice or by appearance. The cadets were clearly identifiable by the fatigues they were wearing, several of the National Guard staff also were dressed in army issue fatigues with "high and tight" haircuts. There was no mistaking this facility with an east coast girls school.

Frank entered the room. Everyone knew immediately this was "the guy." Frank Strupith is the admissions counselor for the Oregon Youth ChalleNGe. His job at the ChalleNGe requires him to be outgoing, personable, and approachable even for and especially regarding youth who question adult authority at every turn. There was no doubt he would be in charge this morning. We would be spending the next 4 hours listening to him carefully and systematically go through the history, entrance requirements, program guidelines, and expectations of the ChalleNGe. He exhibited the confidence you might expect a retired Army veteran of 20 years and a US Army Recruiter Station Commander (E-7 First Class Sergeant) would possess.

Frank walked to the front of the room and rustled a bit with some paperwork and then he purposefully began reaching out to the candidates. One by one he would ask, "So where did you come from this morning?" He did so with a big warm smile, reaching his arm out to shake the hand of the candidate. Oh, there was no doubt who was in control this morning. When each of the candidates answered, he would acknowledge the town and then confidently identify the likely high school they would have attended. As he walked down the line of candidates he was carefully and methodically working the room. I don't mean in a negative way. Clearly, this man understands the importance of first impressions. He knows, I believe, that many of these kids were coming from a place where few authority figures, teachers, and even parents often reached out to them.

In real life, few adults appear to have time to invest in a warm handshake or an inquiring interest to many of these kids. After all, many of these kids have been stereotyped and labeled as troublemakers, deviants, under achievers, and worse. It was obvious that Frank wanted and needed to break through that this morning. After all, these kids were here this morning voluntarily and should they be accepted into the ChalleNGe program, could either accept the invitation or walk away. In fact, no attendee is ever forced to stay at the ChalleNGe and is free to leave at any time.

"Good morning," Frank said to one young man.

"Good morning," the young man, softly speaking, answered back.

"Where did you drive from this morning?" Frank asked.

"Baker City," the young man replied.

"Oh, that is a long drive. Thanks so much for coming all that way today," Frank said.

He continued down the line introducing himself, "Remove your hat young man," Frank politely, but authoritatively, directed one young man.

The young man, quickly and without any reservation, removed his ball cap that I had earlier noticed was positioned on his head in a slightly sideways manner. I must admit, I hate the whole ball cap, worn just a bit off center, exhibited by so many kids today. To me, it defines a person whose life is likely headed in the same direction: sideways. Simplistic, I know. Just my deal.

"Yes sir," the young man said. His cap quickly came off, as did a few others in the room.

As Frank continued working the room, parents mostly sat with their heads down reading the information packs that were distributed by the cadets. The information packets included educational information on grading, coursework, credit hours, and testing. A separate worksheet was included called the "Mentor Brainstorm Worksheet." The worksheet allows for the applicants to consider all adults who may serve as a mentor to the accepted candidates along with the required eligibility standards and ineligibility guidelines.

The room was mostly quiet, except for Frank, who continued welcoming the youth. I could feel the uncomfortableness of parents around me. This isn't the kind of place you dream about coming; but for these parents, it may soon be a place where they would see a complete transformation of their son or daughter and it would surely be a place for which they would become grateful.

It was time for the orientation to officially begin and Frank took control of the room like an entertainer takes control of his stage.

"Ladies and Gentleman, today my goal is to provide you with enough information that you leave here today able to decide if you will want to make application to the ChalleNGe for Class - 34 of 2007 - 2," Frank began.

For the next 4 hours Frank spoke about the 4,000 youths who have gone through the Oregon ChalleNGe; that 60% of attendees enter the ChalleNGe at the 6th grade level in school; that this program has a cost of $17,000 per student, but at no time would any parent be asked to pay for it. He told us how this is a controlled and highly structured environment that changes lives. No phones. No music. No distractions.

"We are a high school, not a military school," he emphasized. "We do *everything* by the numbers here. We march everywhere we go and water is the preferred beverage," he continued. "Some of you today have never lead anything," Frank pronounced as he looked over the group. "If you are accepted into the ChalleNGe program, every one of you will have the opportunity to hold a leadership position," he said firmly. "We will teach each one of you leadership, responsibility, life coping skills, the importance of service to your community, physical fitness, health, hygiene, and academic excellence and job skills," he said as he turned to the presentation screen behind him that displayed the information he had just gone over.

About midway through the orientation presentation, Frank introduced six cadets who were lined up, standing at a position with their legs slightly spread apart, and their hands clinched together behind their backs. He told us that at this point he was inviting all the candidates to go to a separate room where they would have the opportunity to ask the cadets, who had been in the program for about four weeks, any questions.

These cadets had gone through the rigorous two-week boot camp like pre-ChalleNGe and were now well into the program. "The cadets will sit in an open forum-like setting and allow for any questions your son or daughter might have," Frank offered. "Ask the cadets anything you feel will help you in making your decision to come to the ChalleNGe, should you receive an invitation," Frank offered.

At that point he directed the candidates, seated in the first two rows, to follow the cadets to a room in another area of the facility. They walked out the door on the right-hand side of the front area of the room and the door closed behind them. At that point Frank spoke to the adults as.... well, adults, cutting to the chase and making sure the parents understood the principles and guidelines.

I think it might have been the next day when I asked Tony what kind of questions some of the candidates had asked of the cadets. "Do you think they were open and honest?" Tony answered affirmatively. "So, what kind of questions were asked and what were some of the ones that you found important to you?"

Tony replied, "Well, the kids asked questions about what time we had to get up, how hard it was to wake up, can you have tattoos, and one girl asked about being able to wear makeup."

I probed, "So what did you ask, Tony?"

"I asked a couple questions. The first question was, can you write letters to people other than family, like girlfriends? They told us that we will get about forty-five minutes a day to write, dad. So, I guess we are gonna be pen pals."

I laughed and realized, perhaps at that moment, that letters were going to be the only form of communication I was going to be allowed to have for more than five months. No laughing and I guess, no yelling either. "What was the other question, Tony?"

"I asked one of the guys if they liked it here," he replied.

I probed further, "So what did he say?"

Tony answered, "he said this was the hardest thing he had ever done, but he knew that he had to change to have any chance of graduating from high school."

I said to him, "Tony, what I have learned in my business is that many men and women get into the business of real estate to experience change. They might be fed up with their old dead-end job or maybe they had an argument or disagreement with their boss. Some come to me after they have finally realized that there are other opportunities out there and an opportunity to earn a lot of money if they work hard. Unfortunately, most people who come into my office are willing to change only enough to escape their problems.... but not enough of them are willing to fix them. You know that if you are accepted into the ChalleNGe you will be able to escape your problems here for five months; but remember, unless you are willing to face and fix your problems you will never be able to reach your potential. This will be your opportunity. Don't be that person who goes to the ChalleNGe and comes back to do what got you there in the first place, yet expect different results."

Frank was well rehearsed and on his game. He was passionate and took ownership of everything he was saying. This wasn't like the high school I was familiar with. The purpose, Frank's purpose, was *intentional*. I could clearly see that no child would be *allowed* to be skipped over or unattended to by a teacher. *No one* is likely to fall through the cracks here. There was a *commitment to purpose* and *success* that for the first time my son would have the opportunity to experience.

I looked upward at one point. Frank had said that as many as 100 applicants would not be accepted into the ChalleNGe. I have learned in my life that you must first *give* in order to *get*. It is how I have always done business and how I teach my Exit Realty agents; but right now, I had nothing to give and there was no doubt I was hoping to *get* from God at that moment for surely Tony would be lost without this program.

7
ACCEPTED!

Yesterday is not ours to recover, but tomorrow is ours to win or lose.

Lyndon B. Johnson

It was the phone call we were waiting for! When we had attended the ChalleNGe Orientation on March 24th, we were told that we could expect a phone call if (and only if) Tony had been accepted into the program. For three months, we sat and we waited. We prayed and we hoped. We paced and we were full of worry. The next class (2007-2) had a start date of July 19th, and the clock was ticking. But finally, on Monday, June 25th, a call came to Tony.

I remember answering the phone and hearing, "Good afternoon Mr. Mazziotti, this is the Oregon Youth ChalleNGe calling for Anthony Mazziotti. Is he available please?" I remember at the orientation that only those accepted would receive a call. Our prayers had been answered!

"Just one minute please," I replied.

Tony was upstairs in his room. I ran upstairs, phone in hand. While there are only 16 steps to climb to reach the second floor of our home, I was short of breath when I handed the phone to Tony. My heart was pounding and my hands were visibly shaking. I didn't have a mirror to look into, but I am guessing my face was flushed. I walked into Tony's room. The door was cracked open a bit, so no knock was necessary. He was sitting on his bed looking at some papers and he had his headphones on, as I so often found him.

"Tony," I said, "this is the call we have been waiting for." Tony took the phone from me almost hesitantly as I stood above him. He knew who the call was from.

As he put the phone to his ear and said, "Hello?" I could faintly hear, "Good afternoon, Anthony. This is Frank Strupith of the Oregon Youth ChalleNGe. I am calling to inform you that you have been selected for the 2007-2 class commencing on July 19th. You will be receiving a letter in the mail requesting that you confirm your acceptance into the Oregon Youth ChalleNGe. Until then, if you have any questions please feel free to contact me."

The call was over almost as quickly as it had been answered. It was the news we had all be waiting for. I sat down on the edge of his bed, my heart still racing, but now only because of the excitement I was feeling.

I said to him, "this opportunity will only come once, Tony."

"I know, Dad," he replied.

"You are only one defining decision away from a fresh start, Tony," I proffered.

He was almost expressionless. I guess I would have been, too, if the shoe had been on the other foot. Just two weeks after he had completed a horrific junior year in high school and looking, perhaps, at some bit of normalcy that summer vacation offers, he realized that in less than three weeks his summer would end and he would be separated from his family and friends for more than five months.

Honestly, I don't know how I would have handled the news. I have never asked, but I would guess that he placed his face comfortably inside the pillow on his bed and silently cried until he couldn't cry any longer. "How did I get to be in this situation," he must have thought. I know he hadn't been alone in placing himself in this position. There was enough blame to go around. He had been failed by so many: teachers, counselors, coaches, friends, and me.

I walked back downstairs and stepped out onto the front porch of our home. The front porch often provides me with a reasonable amount of privacy and space to sit comfortably and relax or make phone calls. Leann had not arrived home from work, as she often works late in her banking position. I thought about how I might just wait until she arrived home to tell her the news. I guess news like this is better shared one to one, rather than by a phone call. So, I would wait. She should be home shortly. I would wait for her here.

I remember listening to a John C. Maxwell podcast or interview where he said, "In my experience people change when they hurt enough that they have to, they learn enough that they want to, and they receive enough that they are able to." It is like he knew my son. It is like he was sitting on the front porch with me at that very moment.

* * *

The night before Tony left our house, our family decided to all be together so we could share as much time as possible with one another. Nothing was planned, except a day and evening to spend together.

It was a Wednesday night. We spent most of the day and evening finishing up the final details for Tony's departure. Counting the pairs of white socks and white underwear and t-shirts. I have always been given the duty to write the names on the kids' school supplies with a Sharpie and nothing changed on this hot, July night. I remember sitting in my green chair placing his name on everything that was going with him. Unfolding it, marking it, and placing each item carefully into a clear plastic bag. No extras either. We were asked to send along only the allowed and requested and we were alerted to this in the acceptance and admission paperwork. "Any items that are not specific to the supply list given to the candidate will be considered contraband and will be removed from the candidate's belongings." For God's sake, I didn't want to include something in his stuff to get him in trouble on day one.

The time flew by on that day before his leaving for five and one-half months. I knew it would. No matter how I tried to delay time, it passed quickly – too quickly. At about ten o'clock we finally gathered together for one final time in our small living room. No one knew exactly what to say. No one wanted to say the wrong thing. No one really knew what might be the right thing either.

I gave him nudges to remind him that writing would be my priority and I hoped it might be his too, but only if time allowed.

Christiano told him he would write often and make sure he was kept up to date with his remaining baseball season and his upcoming season as a 7th grader on the Sky View Falcons football team.

"You promise me you will play hard, Yanno," Tony said. "Don't take any guff from anyone. You show them who is boss," he concluded.

Leann made sure that he knew we would be available should he need us and that he was only a few miles away.

Nici had learned just a few weeks before Tony left that she had been awarded the fifth-grade teaching position at Vern Patrick Elementary School in Redmond, just 18 miles from our home. She and Tony talked about how she would be near the end of her first semester in her first full year of teaching by the time he returned home. He was curious about her classroom because she had excitedly been looking at photographs for a couple weeks of classrooms and bulletin boards.

"I wish I was here to help you get your classroom ready," Tony said to Nici.

"I'll send you lots of pictures, Tony," she reassured him.

Each time I tried to say something my eyes filled with tears and my throat muscles seemed to contract. I thought it might just be best to save it for the morning.

Once we had determined everything was ready, we set a time to eat breakfast together in the morning at about 6:00 a.m. (early for our family, I would say), and everyone made their way to bed. The two boys and Leann and I each had an officially designated bedroom and Nici, who had returned home after graduating from the University of Northern Iowa, was in the upstairs bonus room. Leann and I remained downstairs to double check everything. I really didn't expect to sleep much, to be honest.

Leann made her way to bed a few minutes before me. Her going allowed me time to think on my own and to contemplate the morning; but once I made my way up the stairs, I quickly took note that both Nici and Christiano's bedrooms had their doors open and each with their beds unoccupied. I opened the door to Tony's room and found the three of them all covered up and in the double bed together.

"You guys alright," I questioned them.

"Dad, we're just gonna hang out together for a while. Would that be okay?"

"Well, okay," I answered back, "but we have to get up in just a few hours and tomorrow is a big day for Tony."

I readied for bed and after a few minutes I joined Leann. As I sat on the side of the bed preparing my alarm clock for the morning, I could hear the kids' muffled voices escape through the bedroom door and down the hall to where I was sitting. These weren't the normal giggles and unruly behavior that you would, under normal circumstances, expect to hear. Instead, their voices were soft, quiet, and consoling. The normal giggle of kids was replaced with the sound of sniffles and blowing noses. My three children, a 24-year old, a 18-year old, and a 13-year old all lay together, each consoling each other. It was heartbreaking and at the same time, heartwarming.

I knew it before, but this assured me of the solidity of the Mazziotti family. Certainly, we were not a perfect family, but our bond and love for one another is strong and authentic. If we could get through this, surely, we could get through anything, right? Only time would tell.

I turned off the light next to my bed where Leann still lay awake and with a huge sigh and release of what seemed to be all the air held in my lungs, lay back, placing the usual three pillows under my head. I slipped my left arm under Leann's head and pulled her as close to me as I could.

"I don't know how I am going to get through this," I said to her.

"I know," she replied back.

"Do you think we are doing the right thing for Tony and for our family," I asked her quietly.

"What else could we do, Jim? There is nowhere else for us to go," she concluded.

"I'm sorry, Leann. There should have been something I could have done to prevent all of this. Maybe I have been too hard on him. Maybe I haven't been hard enough. God knows, I have tried to do the best I could," I confided to her.

Nothing more was said that night. We were too distraught to say anymore to each other and we had covered Tony's long list of failures so many times. Maybe tomorrow would be a new day for him. I mean really a new day.

Before I fell to sleep I thought about how, for so long, Tony had been so troubled and must have been so disappointed in himself, unable to shake all that had become his demons. I thought about something I had heard and I had written down in my journal days earlier.

A lobster, when left high and dry among the rock, does not have the sense enough to work his way back to the sea, but waits for the sea to come to him. If it does not come, he remains where he is and dies, although the slightest effort would enable him to reach the waves, which are perhaps within a yard of him. The world is full of human lobsters; people stranded on the rocks of indecision and procrastination, who, instead of putting forth their own energies, are waiting for some grand billow of good fortune to set them afloat.

Orison Swett Marden (1850 - 1924)

Had I left him high and dry on the rocks? Had I not provided him with everything a young man might need to find safe passage to where he needed to go? Surely, I had to be the one to come and get him and lead him in the right direction, right?

Enough, I thought. There is absolutely nothing and there is no one to save him and I know of no grand billow to set him afloat. I would have to be the one to set him afloat and I would.

But it was the letter Nici sent along with Tony the morning he left that touched my heart when I read from the letters he had brought home and placed in some shoebox months later.

July 18, 2007

Dear Tony,

I'm writing this letter and you are still here, up in your bed fast asleep. I can't imagine how it will be without you here. I know though, that right now you are where you are supposed to be. I can't imagine how hard this is for you and how you are feeling. The only thing I know for sure is how proud I am of you.

Of all the decisions you've made, this one will change your life and that makes me so happy. I am proud that you stepped up to this challenge, and are facing it with a positive attitude.

My hope is that you will stay positive throughout this journey and gain knowledge that you can use throughout your life. You are a fighter Tony; you have always been. That fact lets me know you will make it through this with flying colors. Tony, you can do this. Don't give up. Remember that you have so many people who love you and want nothing more than to see you happy, strong and successful. I love you with all my heart and soul.

Happiness Always,

Nici

Her letter, written on yellow tablet paper was surrounded with short phrases including, "Stay Strong," "I love you!" and "You Can Do This."

The door had been opened for Tony. The ChalleNGe, known as the school of last chances, had just handed him a key. It was his to unlock whichever door he chose…I just hoped it would be the right one.

8

"I'LL BE RIGHT BACK ...I WILL SEE YOU IN A LITTLE WHILE"

All changes, even the most longed for, have their melancholy, for what we leave behind us is a part of ourselves; we must die to one life before we can enter into another.

Anatole France

Today is the day! My heart was broken. I was literally sick to my stomach and hovered over the toilet when I awoke that morning in July, feeling like I would throw up. My stomach churned and turned. I had to get past it and be strong, and I did. I don't know how. Maybe the strength came from above. God knows, I prayed that morning like never before.

I had written out a prayer that I had seen somewhere, made it my own, and tucked away in one of my favorite books I perused often. I slipped the piece of paper with my sloppy handwriting, oddly enough, between page 18 and 19, maybe a clear indication of some OCD issues I have, but it's placement would be easy to remember since it was the 19th day of July, the day Tony would enter the ChalleNGe for five and a half months!

I had actually gone to that book, as I had numerous times these past few months, on the night before he was to leave us and pulled out the piece of paper containing the prayer. I'm not sure how many times I read it as I sat on the side of my bed, upstairs and away from everyone else, but it had to be dozens of times. It seemed like hours, but I know it couldn't have been that long.

On the morning of the 19th, I read it again. I thought, especially on this morning, perhaps I should invite my entire family to recite this prayer together; but I kept it to myself and have to this day. I'm not much for, what I call, rah prayer sessions. Not that I have anything against people praying together, hands in the air, and looking upward. It just isn't me. This was personal and just between God and me.

I opened the book, grabbed the wrinkled and crinkled piece of paper and sat on the edge of my bed, door closed, just me and God. There I read what was written on that piece of paper as I had so many times before. Today, it was even more relevant.

Lord, I would love to be with Tony as he manages the changes in his life.

I would love to hold his hand and whisper words of comfort to him.

I would love to change his situation and bring to him new happiness, confidence and strength. This I know he must do on his own.

I would love to give him peace as he contemplates his future.

I would love to wake him with new hope and inspiration every morning.

I would love to know how to lead him through this very difficult time. Guide me.

I would love to bless him with peace, joy, and hope. God, he needs those things so badly.

You are closer, stronger, wiser than I. No doubt.

You are with him, God.

I ask that you be with Leann, with Nicole, and with Christiano. They are not without pain.

Selfishly, I ask that you be with me today and every day.

I know you are with him and will hold him and protect him today, tomorrow and forever.

I trust in You.

I must trust in You.

Amen

That prayer helped me get through the worst day of my life and doing the best thing I've ever done.

Check-in time at the Oregon Youth ChalleNGe was at 7:00 a.m. I dreaded it for weeks before; but this day had finally arrived. We finished packing the last required items in the clear plastic garbage-like bag that was required for entrance into OYCP, moved about our living room area uncomfortably, mostly not knowing how to act or what to say as the minutes ticked away. I remember the stomach pangs of nerves and heartbreak. I remember having cried most of the prior night, second guessing what we were about to embark upon. Finally, it was time.

The drive to the OYCP facility was a mere 6 miles from our home and that perhaps made it even worse, knowing that within minutes we would be saying goodbye.

"I'll Be Right Back ...I Will See You in a Little While"

It was time.

"Okay," I said. "We had better be going."

Tony stood up, nervously looking at his brother and sister. The awkwardness of the moment was clearly visible on his face and the faces of Nici and Christiano. Nicole, stood first, then Christiano.

Nicole stoically and confidently approached Tony, put her arms around him, and hugged him. "You can do this Tony," she said. "Time will go fast and you are going to learn so much," she continued. "Do this for you, Tony," she said as she released him and wiping away tears.

Then little Christiano. He walked towards Tony, perhaps just a few feet, but the walk seemed more like a mile, I'm sure. As he walked towards Tony, his body shrunk, his shoulders moved inward and downward and he looked mostly towards the floor, his eyes filing with tears. Tony was at least a foot taller than Christiano, but Christiano reached to place his arms around Tony's wide shoulders and began to weep. Then the words Tony spoke, consoling the little brother that forever had looked up to him, I will likely never forget and remain haunting to this day, "I'll be right back. I will see you in a little while."

I don't know why, but those weren't the words I was expecting. He said it so calmly and confidently that if you didn't know Tony was leaving for more than five months, you would think that he might actually be "right back." Yet, we all knew it would be much longer than "a little while." I would have expected him to say just about anything other than that.

Clear sadness filled the room as he picked up his clear plastic bag and made his way for the front door. I think Tony knew he had made the "hard right choice" and that he was about to surrender his own happiness.

Tony walked out of the house, got in our car, and with his mother and me made the 6-mile trip to the OYCP facilities. I could never imagine bringing my son to a place like this. The summer before what was to be his senior year in high school. The year of senior prom, homecoming, football games, and all that makes a kid's senior year the best ever. It wouldn't be so for Tony. *What kind of failure am I anyhow?* I asked myself.

Final reminders of how important this was for his future, the promise that better things would result from this experience, and the assurance that we would always be there for him filled the conversation for this quick trip.

It took only about 10 minutes to arrive from the front door of our home to the parking lot at the Youth ChalleNGe facility. Imagine, just a few months ago, I had never heard of this place, didn't know this facility even existed, and now here I was.

It was 6:34 a.m. There were already a few cars and other parents with their sons or daughters waiting in line for admittance to the five and a half-month program and today's intake. Parents and kids from all over the State of Oregon began to assemble. My heart was pounding through my chest. I felt the pulse from my heart in my throat. I fought back tears and anxiety, as I know my wife, Leann, was also doing. Tony looked around at all the activity, but mostly just stood with his head down staring at the ground.

We stood in line as more cars entered the parking lot and more parents or guardians taking the walk, many hand in hand or arms around one another. There wasn't any laughter or joy anywhere that I could see. If there might have been, I am sure it would have been manufactured out of nervous anticipation. This was serious. Just a lot of fear of the unknown and the reality of it all. I remember thinking of a quote I couldn't quite put together that morning or even who said it, but later searched for it and found the words of actress, Taraji P. Henson, who said, "Every human walks around with a certain kind of sadness. They may not wear it on their sleeves, but it's there if you look deep." Trust me, I didn't have to look deep today.

Sadness was everywhere. And I for one, along with many others, were wearing our sadness on our sleeves.

As I looked at the young "candidates" I thought, how is it that my son is here with…with…" these kids." I mean, give me a break. My son, a proud Mazziotti boy? Let me be honest. Some of the parents and kids had "it" written all over them. Their clothes, the cars they drove, the multicolored hair styles, the saggy-butt pants, the tattoos; you know – all the politically incorrect opinions – yes, I was feeling. Not my kid. My kid doesn't belong here with "these kids." He is better than "them." But the fact was, we were here and not because he had done all the right things, or frankly, because I had done all the right things.

You could almost smell trouble. The typical politically incorrect judgments encompassed my every thought. We are a typical middle-class family and some of "these people" drove up in cars that you know barely had enough tread on the tires or gas in the tanks to make the journey. Some looked as if they just got out of bed and were wearing the same clothes they slept in. You just knew for some of these folks it took divine intervention to have ever convinced their son or daughter that this was the right place to be. Some brought brothers and sisters or boyfriends or girlfriends along for the orientation.

At exactly 7:00 a.m. the doors opened and about 60 candidates, their parents and family, were all guided carefully to a large room. We all crowded into the room, sizeable enough to comfortably hold 150 or so people. To get to the room we were lead though this very cold and sterile building of narrow hallways with small offices and doors off to each side. I don't remember seeing anyone in the offices, but I am sure staff was there. I was overwhelmed. I was stunned. It was apparent this wasn't anything like home.

The three of us made our way to the very front row seating area, slightly right of a presentation podium. I wanted to be sure to catch every word from whomever was going to speak to us. I didn't want to miss one detail of what would be happening today and for the next 154 days, what was expected from Tony, and what the expectations were for his mother and me. We were told this meeting would last about two and one-half hours for the orientation and in-processing.

The room began to fill slowly while all those who were waiting outside with us made their way in. I could hear instructions to some of the parents being given in Spanish by one or two of the staff members. Parents and guardians had received detailed instructions in late June as to what to bring, such as proof of insurance, social security numbers, credit or debit cards to establish a Safeway store account (for prescription refills and other supplies that might be needed), and maybe the most important – a minimum of five letters written in advance for their child. I knew that I had already written a letter and mailed it a couple days before, but for some reason I don't recall writing five letters to leave at the facility. Maybe because I knew mail would likely take just one day since our post office was only 7 miles away and I knew I wasn't going to miss even one day to write to Tony.

As we sat waiting for this first day of intake to begin, it seemed apparent, to me at least, that the single most important requirement to be accepted into the OYCP might be unobtainable for many of the kids. In the paperwork, it clearly stated, "As a candidate, you are subject to a mandatory urinalysis drug screen. If you fail the drug screen, you will be sent home today!"

Listen, I wasn't born yesterday. We knew that applicants, including Tony, were labeled as "at risk." They wouldn't be here if they weren't. At risk can mean a lot of things; but as I looked around me I identified, in my judgmental mind, that more than a few of the attendees in the room would test positive for drugs. I looked at Leann and quietly whispered, "How many kids do you think will be going home today?" She knew what I was asking. I was confident that Tony hadn't

"I'll Be Right Back ...I Will See You in a Little While"

used drugs and alcohol, so I didn't give it a second thought. I couldn't imagine how despondent a parent would be if they were told to grab their child and leave.

I looked at my watch as the time was approaching the 7:30 a.m. start. I could feel perspiration running down my back and I knew it wasn't especially warm in the room, even with 300 or so people. As I scanned the room from front to back, I had a sense of who would be speaking to us today. A man approached the podium and introduced himself.

Those in the room included OYCP Cadre who were wearing their Army National Guard fatigues. They stood, clearly maintaining command and demonstrating their authority. They moved about with perfect posture, shoulders back, and there was no doubt who was in charge. If the candidates and their parents were not clear before, they certainly were at this point. They were standing in the back of the room against the wall and along the right-hand side of the room, which included two entry/exit doors. Also in attendance were men and women in casual business attire, much like you would see any teacher wearing in the average American school and I gathered they were, in fact, the teachers. The OYCP has four teachers who work in the classroom setting and who do not participate in the intense physical training and discipline requirements expected from each candidate. Those are handled by the cadre.

"Good morning ladies and gentleman. Welcome to The Oregon Youth ChalleNGe Facility."

It now became real.

The Director of the Oregon Youth ChalleNGe, Mr. Dan Radabaugh, took the floor in front of the room. He was dressed professionally and he stood confidently and in charge.

For the better part of 90 minutes, the program's uniqueness and a clear description of what the next five and a half months would hold were explained with precision. This clearly wasn't the first rodeo for the officials from The ChalleNGe.

Every detail was covered. Paperwork was placed in our hands and I found myself franticly taking notes. Dates, times, and details were scribbled on the tops and bottoms of the pages and when I would run out of room, I found additional space in the margins, writing from top to bottom. I didn't want to miss a thing. My normally wandering mind was honed in and focused on every syllable of every word that was spoken. Occasionally, I leaned over to Leann to verify something that had been said that either wasn't clear to me or that I didn't hear correctly while madly making notes.

About midway through the presentation, the director instructed all the candidates to make their way to another room where they would have the opportunity to speak and ask questions from past graduates of the program, who had returned for the day to "give back" to those entering the program and to tell of their experiences while at OYCP. Facility staff was also there to answer any procedural or program questions. The kids all stood from their seats and walked to the front of the room and they very orderly, and in single file entered the adjoining room to the front right-side of the room.

Upon the last candidate walking through the door, the door closed and the room was left with just parents, guardians, family, and the director of the program. "Ladies and Gentlemen," Mr. Radabaugh said, "your sons and daughters will be in the next room for less than an hour. There they will be able to ask anything and they will. Any question, every question, will be answered today. So, while they are separated from us, we will cover details of your child's journey the next 154 days." Everything was covered. Questions from parents and guardians were addressed and handled.

"Now, Mr. Radabaugh said, "when your sons and daughters come back into the room we are going to finish up with some program instructions and you will be dismissed. As I dismiss the candidates please say goodbye as calmly as you can and leave them with a sense of confidence that you know they will succeed and that you support them. Your support of your child and of this program are so important."

Minutes later the door opened at the front of the room and the kids came in, quietly, and resumed their seats, most of whom were next to their mothers or fathers. Then, after a brief moment or two and with abruptness and no warning, the director, in a firm and commanding voice said, "Parents and candidates, the time has come. Please stand, hug your sons/daughters and quickly say goodbye.

At that moment, cadre, dressed in military fatigues moved quickly up each side of the room and began barking and shouting for the candidates to depart and move forward. It was like the storm troopers from Star Wars had suddenly appeared to demonstrate superiority and command. And they did. The kids, completely caught by surprise, as were we, shuffled and gathered about, some stumbling while making their way in the direction of the shouting cadre.

"Move it! I said move it!" was heard from one cadre. "Let's go people! Pick up your belongings and let's go," barked another.

The faces of the kids turned from carefree and disinterested to fearful, dismayed, surprised, and panicked! Chills filled my body. I looked around feeling many of those same emotions. One minute we were slowly and passionately hugging Tony, stroking his head as we embraced and like a shot out of a canyon, he was almost ripped from our arms and whisked away. *Oh my God, is this it?* It was. Tony quickly moved towards the exit door along with the others, in single file, and in a matter of seconds disappeared from our view. He was gone.

As Leann and I gathered our thoughts, turning away from the door where Tony has just walked out, I remember looking at her, directly into her eyes, seeing astonishment and bewilderment. I'm guessing she saw the same in mine. "Did this just happen, Leann," I said to her. She was speechless and not responding to me, merely looking away and taking in the emotions of others in the room. Other family's emotions were not unlike those we were feeling as well. Tears were abundant. The hiccupping sound of crying reverberated from around of the room. Supportive hugs and embraces remained, while others had and continued to make their way out of the room, down the hallway and out the front of the building to the parking lot.

I told Leann I was going to personally approach the director and thank him for giving Tony the opportunity to change his life. In retrospect, I should have grabbed Leann and put my arms around her, giving her some kind of assurance that everything was going to be okay. I should have whispered into her ear, telling her how much I loved her. I didn't. That was a mistake. I should have. I seldom did. That also, was a mistake. Remember the "tiny moments?" Reflecting back, this was a moment that I should have shown how much I loved her.

9
THE FIRST OF OUR 144 LETTERS

Things don't go wrong and break your heart so you can become bitter and give up. They happen to break you down and build you up so you can be all that you were intended to be.

Charlie Jones

At the orientation event, weeks before intake, the parents and guardians of accepted candidates were asked to write a letter to our son or daughter and send it with them on 'intake day,' the first day of The ChalleNGe. I wrote the first letter that accompanied Tony to The ChalleNGe on Wednesday, July 11th.

In that very first letter I spoke of those things that I thought might touch his heart and provide him with comfort. Maybe they were words that were providing more comfort to me, to be honest. I wanted him to know that "those tiny moments" had, in fact, had a significant impact on my life and would never be forgotten. I thought how writing letters in the coming days, weeks, and months would give me the opportunity to look back and relive many wonderful moments, as well as the roadblocks and disappointments we had faced. *How many of us are given that opportunity?*

While I might remember these "tiny moments" from time to time, this experience would give me a special opportunity to dissect the moments in my mind and relive them again; to smell the smells of Wrigley Field in Chicago during a hot summer game while sitting together in the bleacher seats, just him and me; to speak of the fear I felt when sitting atop the Ferris Wheel at Navy Pier, the 150-feet high ride that stands tall above everything else on the Pier and that was as an exact replica of the original Ferris Wheel built for the Chicago 1893 World Columbian Exposition; remembering that it took forever just to make one rotation at a height that seemed to be high enough to reach out and touch the top of Chicago's famous Sears Tower, the tallest building in America at that time!

In my first letter, I wrote, "There are so many great 'tiny moments,' Tony. The moment when we sat atop navy Pier in Chicago on what I think may be America's largest Ferris Wheel. God! I was scared; but I was with you. It was just you and me. No one could touch us. No one could come between us. I'll never forget that moment."

As I wrote, I remember my fingers tapping out each word …slowly….and from time to time closing my eyes to visualize that moment. I pressed my eyes tighter and tighter, thinking that concentration might enhance the picture I was seeing in my mind. My chest was hurting and my eyes filling with tears. I wondered if I had taken that moment and hundreds, maybe millions of others, for granted. I realized, like many of us, I had taken them for granted. I swore I would never take another "tiny moment" for granted ever again. Not now. Not after all of this.

I stopped typing and I sat patiently with my eyes closed. I sat and found, almost like magic, that by doing so, I could actually see the two of us riding the chartered bus, full of mostly older members from our small Iowa community, to make the 250-mile trip to Chicago. I could see Leann dropping us off in the south parking lot at the waiting Hawkeye Stages blue and white bus, she holding Christiano and watching us put our suitcases in the travel compartment underneath the big bus. Tony got to take his very own suitcase for this trip and it was a big deal that he and I were going away like big boys for a very long adventure of three whole days! The two of us climbing up the bus stairs and walking down the aisle to find our seats and passing familiar faces, all seemingly with big smiles on their faces anticipating the special adventure and the opportunity to go to the big city and watch the Cubs.

Some people stopped whatever they were doing to take notice of Tony. He was easily the youngest attendee and surely the cutest. I could see some of those familiar faces patting him on top of his head, which was, of course, adorning a slightly worn blue cap with a big red "C" on the front, while we made our way to near the rear of the bus. After all, that is where he said he wanted to sit.

This trip was known as "The Vic Gallo Chicago Cubs Trip." It was easily one of the top summer attractions in our small town for approximately 50 lucky people who could afford the $99 price for the one night/two-day trip that would allow each to watch three games: one single game, and one doubleheader. I recall the image of Vic welcoming Tony as we got on the bus. Vic, a retired newspaper man, was a gregarious old Italian gentleman. If you didn't know him and only judged him on his looks, you might incorrectly think he was an old unfriendly, cold, and harsh man; but he was just the opposite. Tony took a liking to Vic and spent much of the bus-trip helping him with some easy assignments that primarily involved helping Vic with the games and pools he created to entertain the passengers on this five-hour bus-trip. I could see Tony's face light up whenever Vic would call out his name. Tony's big smile, with a couple spaces opened up where his baby teeth were missing; his lanky body moving easily throughout the aisles to pick up whatever special prize Vic had prepared.

Now, as I wrote, memories began to flood my mind. As I continued to keep my eyes closed, I could visualize both good and bad. Some things for only a brief moment and others for longer. I wrote about those.

> *I remember the joy of seeing you hit the ball and running the bases when you were playing for the Kings Knights. And I remember how aggravated I was when you were ignoring the game while you were playing left field. The batter was up for the other team and almost certainly the ball would be coming to you if the batter managed to hit it....and there you were, like nothing else mattered except you're watching the grass fly through the air as you picked it and flung it over your head.*
>
> *I will never forget the feeling I would experience on those days where I picked you up from daycare. Seeing the excitement in your eyes when you saw me and having your arms wrapped around me as we would walk out the door to go home.*
>
> *The sorrow and the joy of moving to Bend. Seeing you cry as we said goodbye to our family and many friends. The time we spent riding together, just you and I for hundreds of miles as we made our way west across the United States and the joy and anticipation of seeing our new home, the mountains, and your new school.*

Now, as I continued to write, I changed from seeing us together in the past to now anticipating what it would be like at his new home for more than five months. Again, I closed my eyes and I wrote to him what I was seeing.

The First of Our 144 Letters

Here you are. I am guessing as I write this first letter to you that you will be reading this while sitting on your bunk after a long and very difficult day. Am I right, Tony? I would guess you are wondering what we are doing at home...right now...as you read this letter.

As I put those words on paper I selfishly began to anticipate what that first day would be like for me and our family, but mostly me. *Damn, how on earth will I be able to get through this?* As I thought and visualized what I anticipated for the months ahead, I decided it might be important for him to know all that was going on in my mind. I wanted him to know, through my letter and subsequent letters, that he would not be alone. Not for one minute. Not for one second. So, I began to scratch out on paper those anticipated thoughts. All together there were 56 things I wrote down and put into the letter. I wrote:

So, Tony, let me give you some idea of what many of my 'little moments' will likely be like while you are gone. I will be thinking...is Tony okay today. I wish I could see Tony. Is God dishing out more than Tony can handle? I bet Tony misses his friends. I wonder if Copper is lonely too. I bet Tony is showing everyone what a smart and great kid he is. Christiano sure misses Tony...and we all do. I wish I could yell upstairs in frustration that you won't get up! Today is the first day of school of Tony's senior year...I just wish Tony was here and could walk to school today. Did we do the right things? Has Tony seen the light? I hope Tony can sleep tonight? There sure wasn't much laundry today. Is there something I could have done better for Tony? Tony gets to come home today for a brief visit...I hope we can make his stay enjoyable...I can't wait to see him, to hug him, to feel him, to smell him...and to laugh with him and just have him home. I bet Tony will win numerous leadership awards…that is, if he wants to. I can hear the crowd cheering just a few blocks away at the Mountain View football game…I bet Tony would be there if he were home. It is snowing…I wonder if Tony has to be outside today. Man, the Mountain View basketball team needs him tonight ….it really is no fun going to the games without seeing him and all his friends. Mom sure misses Tony. It won't be long now. I hope we can make this the best Christmas ever for Tony and our family. My final visualization was my best and managed to cut through the tears. It was of me calling out to Leann saying, "Leann…come on…it's time to pick Tony up. He is coming home today!"

As I finished up this very first letter I asked him to take time to dream.

Tony, the indispensable first step of getting what you want out of life is to decide what you really want. Part of this experience is to find out, not only who you are… but to decide what you want. What you REALLY want. So, as you finish reading this first letter, know that I am proud of you for taking the step to accept this ChalleNGe….and know I am proud of you. I have never been prouder. Know that while you are reading this letter I will be somewhere thinking of you and missing everything about you. Nothing can change how much I love and care about you.

* * *

I don't recall, specifically, what had transpired on the day I wrote this letter, but I do know that I wanted more for myself and my business. Even though I was only several months into my business, I also had dreamed to shoot higher than I thought possible. Yet, I can honestly say that I was focused

The First of Our 144 Letters

a bit on working to be better than my contemporaries and predecessors. When I made the move nearly 2,000 miles from my hometown I did so for exactly that reason. I thought I had much to prove to everyone and to myself. Let's face it, I was in the half of my high school class that made the top half possible. I would wager that few, if any, of my teachers in high school thought for a minute I would lead my own real estate company one day.

I will never forget the day I told my ailing mother that I was selling the family music business. Without hesitation she responded, "but Jim...you can't do anything else." She wasn't demeaning or insulting. She simply uttered what she was thinking at that moment. I would bet, if my father would have been alive, he would have said the same thing and questioned the rationale behind the decision.

So, I had something to prove. I did want to shoot higher; and yes, I wanted to show anyone who doubted my abilities to succeed that they were wrong. However, I wasn't exactly lighting it up. Yet, no one could question my days revolving around shooting higher and helping the agents who had made the investment in coming to my company do the very same.

Damnit! I know Tony is facing the same thing. There are teachers at his school and perhaps friends and their parents who think he is a lost cause – the nice boy that is a low achiever – they are thinking. In fact, my guess would be, with the exception of his mentor and former teacher, Joe Padilla, not one teacher or counselor will give him one rat's ass of a thought the first day of school. I think that could be the story of the other 156 kids that entered into the Oregon Youth ChalleNGe on day one and with every subsequent class after and in the future.

For me, it was my hope that my first letter, likely read in his bunk after a long and grueling day, would provide him with a sense of the love we felt for him and help him move forward. I felt it was important to prepare Tony as best as I could for the coming months in my letters to him.

10
THE PROMISE

*As you go about your day, know this…at times during the day
I am thinking of you…I mean…really thinking about you.
I hope you can feel it…. You are not alone.*

As Leann and I arrived home at about 10:30 a.m. or so, both Nicole and Christiano were anxiously awaiting our return and they were both sitting on the couch watching television. As we walked through the front door, Nicole grabbed the remote control and muted the volume and looked to us anticipating. Both Leann and I had planned to take this Thursday off from work, so we were able to sit with them and share with them how the morning had gone for Tony. We spent the next hour or so just talking about how we could all best handle our own sadness and, in the midst of that, provide support for Tony knowing that the first two weeks of Pre-ChalleNGe would be the toughest two weeks of his life and the lives of 156 other young boys and girls.

I was mostly lost at this point, not knowing exactly what to do. The four of us sat, without knowing what to say or what questions to ask of each other. I couldn't stop thinking about the two minutes we were given, quite unexpectedly, to say goodbye to Tony and then have the Cadre turn from quiet spectators to screaming, angry, yelling drill instructors! To see the look of horror on most of the kid's faces when ORDERED to move quickly to the front of the room. To hear the sound of the west front door slamming behind the youth once all the candidates had left the presentation room. The voices of the Cadre screaming commands heard through the walls, much louder than you might expect to hear and with undistinguishable, yet powerful voices. What could Tony have thought at that moment? What could he be thinking now?

Not knowing what else to do, I checked in with Carly, my secretary, to see if there were any calls that needed attention and to describe to her what the morning had been like. Thankfully, there were no calls to return nor agents to consult.

While I had demonstrated my vulnerability to sadness through tears, neither Leann, Nicole, nor Christiano really had any idea just how broken I was, on this, my 53rd birthday. *Dammit, what could I have done differently? Now, what do I do?* The only therapy I could think of was to express to Tony how much I loved him and how proud I was that he agreed to apply for and commit to this program and to do so by writing letters from my heart on a daily basis. Every day.

I promised myself I would write a letter to Tony every single day. That was my mission. I knew he would be homesick. No music allowed. Virtually no talking permitted. No computers and absolutely no cell phones. The poor lonely kid. So, what would I say in my letters to Tony? I mean, I have no idea what he will be experiencing at The ChalleNGe. Our lives here at home are so mundane, I mean, writing a letter every day?

I decided that I would build my letters upon the words of wiser men and women, relying on their inspiration to motivate, inspire, and strengthen him, and me as well. I am a student of many inspirational business coaches and speakers: Zig Ziglar, John C, Maxwell, Brian Tracy, Les Brown, Napoleon Hill, and so many others. Let's face it, at the very moment I was looking for ways to inspire Tony, I was also looking deep inside of me and trying to figure out how the words of others might inspire me and move me. Maybe in my letter writing to Tony I could also strengthen my own spirit to take on the incredible challenges of a real estate market that had begun to see its demise, and I was feeling it.

* * *

I opened my Exit Realty franchise office on the anniversary of the Exit Realty Corporation International's 10-year anniversary. The day was special, but opening on the anniversary of our company's founding was the icing on the cake. However, as soon as I opened, almost overnight, the incredible boon that Bend had been experiencing in real estate had begun to tumble out of control.

The Bend, Oregon, area had, and continues to receive, accolades from major news and lifestyle publications for years. Everywhere you turned you could read or hear about the superb restaurants, the marvelous galleries, some of the top golf courses in the world carrying the signatures of the game's greatest names like Fazio, Nicklaus, and Cupp. Being located at the foothills of the glorious Cascades, Bend boasted stunning evergreen forests to the west and the high desert grasslands to the east and is home to one of the world's most beautiful ski and snowboarding mountains in America, as well as world-class biking, hiking, fishing, climbing ... the list goes on. So, for heaven's sake, how could the real estate market ever implode?

It did.

The first quarter of 2007 came and oh my! CNN/Money reported that National City Corporation and Global Insight found that Bend, Oregon, was the most overvalued metro in the nation. They pointed out that the median single-family home price was $324,000, almost twice what it sold for just four years earlier and 78.7% over the surveys valuation price. In 2005, Bend was ranked the sixth fastest-growing metropolitan area in the country by the U.S. Census Bureau. Now, we were the headliner in America for everything awful about real estate … and I was in head first.[1]

When opening my Bend office, I literally brought every last dime I had to the table to open my franchise. Savings, insurance policies, family, refinancing my home, and even searching my accounts receivable files from our family music business that I had sold more than a decade earlier. I was all in. Now, here I was watching an almost certain fate in my business and the simultaneous failure of my son not being able to go on to his senior year in high school.

So maybe the letters to my son would build my inner strength while building his. Is it possible we could both survive this crisis?

I went to my bookshelf and pulled down the book, mostly covered with dust, *Wherever You Go, There You Are*, by Jon Kabat-Zinn. I remembered purchasing and reading this book with my mother, who looked to it for ways to remove the stress and pain of her battle with terminal lung cancer. His technique of mindfulness meditation was intended to help people reduce stress, deal with chronic pain, and a variety of illnesses, particularly breast cancer. Perhaps, there was advice within its pages that might reduce my stress. In fact, once I opened the book I remembered Karat-Zinn had been a trainer for the 1984 USA Men's Olympic Rowing Team, so perhaps his words would be welcome to Tony on that first day.

As I began to turn the wrinkled pages, that had at one time apparently seen a water, or more appropriately, a soda spill, my eyes fell upon words that immediately connected with me.

---

[1] In an article on 2/26/12, Elon Glucklich from the Bend Bulletin wrote that by the end of 2009, Bend prices had dropped 68% from their 2007 value

The little things? The little moments? They aren't little.

This quote gave me a starting point for my very first letter to Tony and maybe the key to enter his heart and to release the pain from mine. I wanted Tony to know that I hadn't taken the little moments lightly. I now realized I valued every moment I had ever spent with him.

I also realized I would not be there to share in his little moments while he was away and I began to ponder what moments he might experience in the next five and a half months and whether he would have time to reflect on those we had shared. I ended up writing more than 50 moments. I wanted him to know I would be praying that he wasn't too hot or too cold. I needed for him to know I understood he would be lonely, homesick, sore from required and extended exercise mandates, homesick for his mother's pasta, and that time would likely move slow while anticipating his first home visit.

As I studied every morsel of information I could find about the OYC I knew that his first day would be the hardest of his life, followed by two weeks of non-stop discipline, structure, and a military-like boot camp atmosphere. While the facility is a "hands off" home for youth from all 36 counties of Oregon, I clearly understood that the cadre (cadre or team leaders, who directly supervise all daily activities of the cadets) would immediately take charge of Tony in what I call a "Marine Drill Instructor" mentality from the very first minute upon entrance. He was about to be part of one of the most intense alternative schools in the country.

The will to succeed is important, but what is even more important is the will to prepare.

I had studied the Youth ChalleNGe Program inside and out. I sought to find information wherever I could. Thankfully, the Internet allows for thorough research on just about anyone or any organization. So, I knew going in exactly what was in store for Tony.

The first two weeks of the ChalleNGe is a preparatory period for making sure all the candidates knew who was calling the shots and exactly what was in store for them over the next several months.

I felt it was important to help prepare Tony as best as I could for the coming months in my letters to him. Each letter was filled with what anyone might include in their letters to a son or daughter. I spoke about what was going on at home. I talked about how Christiano and Nic were doing. I tried to offer a picture in words of the daily events that he had witnessed many times or could easily see us doing in the course of a day: simple mentions of what we had for dinner or where we had gone for the evening or the day; how extended family members were doing in Iowa and in Portland; I even joked about the terrible couch that we often called "the valley of death," since surely, anyone who sat on it would end up being eaten by the worn-out cushions and non-springy springs. It was summer, so there weren't any school functions or games to tell him about.

In my third letter to him I emphasized a quote. I wanted him to be able to hear inspiration that he probably hadn't bought into before, because, perhaps, he hadn't felt the need to do so. I reaffirmed in my next few letters how the first weeks, the hardest he will have ever experienced, were designed to help him prepare for what would make him successful, not only at The ChalleNGe, but for the remainder of his young life.

To help him understand that quotes are something more than mere words or fashionable explanations of life, I tried, with almost every letter, to correlate them in real examples, usually to my life or to my business. The Bobby Knight quote allowed me to show him that, just like his need to prepare at the ChalleNGe, I also had a need to prepare almost daily in order to achieve. *Isn't it true that I had to inspire and assist all those working for me to prepare?*

I had learned long ago that my path and the path chosen by real estate agents like me, don't offer the advantages of what many would call a comfortable job. You know the jobs of which I speak. The ones offering stable constant hours, a specific job duty, and guaranteeing a check every two weeks and the ability to perhaps climb the ladder as reward for a job well done. That is what I call a traditional job. I think there are fewer of these types of jobs available these days; but nevertheless, they still exist. That's not what I had. I had what I had seen some authors and business guru's call an Inspirational Job. A job built on the ability to take it anywhere I wanted it to go, based on a vision to achieve, with a huge growth and income potential, and the ability to create my very own product, but also with the realization that I held all the strings. No one else had the ability to pull the strings to make things happen for me. So, I wanted him to know that like me, he needed to take this time to prepare as he dreamed.

I believe in dreaming. Maybe I always have. Perhaps, too much so for the teachers who experienced my dreaming almost constantly throughout the day when a school child. Most children first see themselves through the eyes of their parents, teachers, and other role models. I guess I was one of those children for the most part.

I sat down in my green chair and reached for my computer, where I have, for many years, gathered favorite quotes and motivational thoughts, and found one from Charles "Tremendous" Jones which I thought best described what Tony would be facing for the next five and a half months.

Things don't go wrong and break your heart so you can become bitter and give up. They happen to break you down and build you up so you can be all that you were intended to be.

That was it! As I look back, this quote was as much for me as it was Tony. Yes, my real estate business, like Tony's life, was in trouble, but there was no way I was going to go down without fighting. I was going to demonstrate to every real estate agent and every office, both dropping like flies by closing their offices or taking part time jobs, doing almost anything they could for work and even committing suicide, that I was going to succeed. *God dammit, nothing was going to prevent me from being my best self.* I wanted to make sure there was no quit in Tony!

I began to write. I wanted him to know that we were his cheerleaders and with him more than ever. I know he had heard all we told him, but I also knew he would hear it through a different filter through my letters. Throughout the ages, letters have changed people's lives and in the process, the course of history. I could only hope mine would do the same.

Day #1 July 19th, 2007

Tony,

Well, today truly was one of the hardest and most difficult days of my life. And today was one of a special excitement too! It is difficult to explain.... but let me try.

My stomach has been tied up in knots for a long time. We have had our challenges trying to always keep you on the right track...heck, every parent does. That is nothing unusual. But the knot has been especially tight the past four months. The knot became especially tight the day I drove alone out to OYC. I just didn't know what to do... how to help you...so I got in my car and drove out there. I didn't tell your mother or anyone else for that matter. Once there I was even more confused...but I knew this "is a place of second chances." You deserve a second chance.

You are one of the best young kids I have ever known. I knew you needed help from what you were going through at Mountain View...not that I could explain it or understand it.... but I knew it. But that is when the knot started tightening up. It's been a long few months.

And today. Looking at you. Looking at the other boys. Looking at you again. Back and forth. And while my heart hurts right now I just know you are going to lead the way for many of those around you. It's in you, Tony. You are kind, generous, smart and outgoing. You really have it all! But geez...letting go. Not seeing you every day (or almost every day) for most of the last 18 years! I bet the longest time I have spent away from you has been when you were at the Cascade Basketball Camp or maybe when I had to travel to Toronto or Orlando for this EXIT thing.

But I am excited. You are going to do fantastic! You are going to be a better man after this. You are going to be a better student. You are going to be a better friend. This is your time. IT IS YOUR TIME. God has a plan for you... he really does. Accept it. But man, I am going to miss you.

And yes...right now my heart hurts...but I know it's going to be okay, it's going to be a great experience for you. I know it!

> *Things don't go wrong and break your heart so you can become bitter and give up. They happen to break you down and build you up so you can be all that you were intended to be."*
>
> *Charles "Tremendous" Jones*
> *Speaker and Author*

The Promise

Yep! I believe it. You will too. What you are going through right now is a tested plan at OYC. They don't put you through the 2-Week Pre-ChalleNGe because they think it might work. Nope. They KNOW IT WORKS. Just like it says in the quote.... they are breaking you down to your CORE and are going to put the bricks on and build you back up. You'll see.

Know this. As hard as it was for each one of us. Mom, Nici, Yanno, I (and Copper too) .... we all BELIEVE IN YOU. We do. We are your cheerleaders. We always have been your cheerleaders if you think about it. And we are with you more and more than ever.

And this morning you said something powerful. I mean, really powerful......and you said it perhaps without really thinking about it! As you hugged your little brother and big sister you said, "I'll be right back...I'll see you in a little while." Damn! That was powerful to hear Tony! That is the kind of attitude that will allow you to fly through this experience with flying colors.... and you will. I'll never forget you saying that to Nici and Yanno. Sometimes you say just the right things.

"I love you dad...I'll be okay."

All I can say is thanks for those words to me as you hugged me. And I know you will be okay! I'll be okay too, Tony. I am so proud of your taking this challenge!

"See You In 43 Days"

(even less by the time you get this letter)

But who's counting? I am. As I am writing this letter it'll be just 43 days until the Labor Day Break! That is fantastic. No Chinese Buffet! Anything...anything... but that! Maybe you would like to go to Portland or something...or maybe just chill. So, I've got the calendar with your picture on my wall. I have circled and highlighted the day's we get to see you....and we will be there the minute they allow you to come home...just waiting! And best of all.... December 19th. Just 153 days from now!

So, as you said.... "I'll be right back.... I'll see you in a little while!"

We love you!

Dad

The first "official" letter was complete. I folded it, placed it in an envelope, walked over to the desk, placed a stamp on it, placed it in my back pocket so that it was partially exposed but safely tucked away and I told Leann and the kids that I was going for a walk.

Christiano jumped out of the chair he was sitting in and was quickly at my side as I walked out the front door. "Hey dad," he said, "can I go for a walk with you?"

"Sure, but I'm not going far, Christiano. Just to the mailbox and back," I replied.

"Can I take Copper, dad," he asked as we were walking down the front steps.

"Sure," I told him. "But hurry up!"

The neighborhood was quiet. Most of the neighbors in our neighborhood are working people. I guess there are a few retired folks here and there, but I knew that our walk would likely not require me to say hello to anyone or exchange niceties along the way. I really was in no mood to talk.

As I walked at a reasonably slow pace, Christiano and his dog quickly caught up to me and were in their own world, as most 12 year olds often are. The dog wasn't cooperating and was pulling Christiano from side to side and sniffing every tree, bush, and blade of grass on our two-block journey. I thought about what I had just written, hoping that I said the right things and the things Tony needed to hear.

I arrived at the mailbox with Christiano and Copper now a half a block behind me. This would be the first of many deliveries of the letters to Tony.

11
THE LETTERS

The nature of the epistolary genre was revealed to me: a form of writing devoted to another person. Novels, poems, and so on, were texts into which others were free to enter, or not. Letters, on the other hand, did not exist without the other person, and their very mission, their significance, was the epiphany of the recipient.

Amélie Nothomb, *Life Form*

The word that is heard perishes, but the letter that is written remains.

- Proverb

I walked into my office on Friday, July 20th, the day after leaving Tony at The ChalleNGe with no sense of urgency to do anything. The truth is, I had left home about an hour early so that I could drive out to the Oregon Youth ChalleNGe facility to see if I might catch a glimpse of Tony or something. The "something," I guess, was just knowing I was close to him. You know the feeling. It is like taking a child to the park playground and walking away, not far, but just far enough away so that your child can experience their own independence and world of play, yet knowing you are just steps away from saving the day should he or she slip and fall or need special encouragement and support to take that next step, climb up the slide that you know must look like the height of a building to them. Surely, I wouldn't be able to reach out to Tony.

As I sat down at my desk I turned my swivel chair towards the large window that looks out upon Greenwood Avenue, one of, if not the busiest business street in Bend. My desk sits slightly away from the wall to my right with plenty of space to come and go from the left side when I exit my chair. The wall on my right is littered with lots of stuff: schedules, important contacts with phone numbers and emails, floor plans for office lease space that I manage, business cards of key contacts, and a few pictures. I leaned back, took a breath and decided to just relax and take time to think.

I had purposely not scheduled anything for "the day after." So, unless one of my real estate agents came in requiring my assistance, I knew I could direct my attention to doing whatever I might need to do. My secretary, Carly, had asked much earlier for the day off, and frankly, I was relieved that I did not have to talk to her or anyone else about the day prior. I was content just having the time to think in a quiet office. Actually, I wanted to be alone. I needed to be alone.

I keep time blocking accountability sheets on my desk. I had incorporated the habit of writing daily goals for the day when working with my real estate coach, Rich Rudnick, for a brief period in late 2006. His coaching encompassed tracking just about everything. We worked on setting goals, plans to operate and build my business, strategies to increase production and we even looked at the attitudes and mindsets needed to be successful. He helped support me in believing in myself, believing in my product and service, in favoring quality over quantity, in possessing enthusiastic optimism, in believing I would succeed, that risk has its reward, and the need to live "on purpose."

As I looked at my "to do" list for the day, I had scheduled time to make a calendar that would track each day and that would allow me to countdown when, where, and what Tony would be doing during the next 156 days. I decided I would place this customized calendar on the wall next to my desk in a space I had cleared out for its display.

As I constructed the calendar, I first placed numbers on each dated block. The numbers counted backwards so each day I would know how many days it would be until Tony would finally be home. I started: 156…155….154…and so on. I knew that watching the days pass by would provide me with the enthusiasm and gratitude that I would need. I realized it might also remind me of the agony of waiting… counting… agonizing. As I worked on the calendar I made a point to mark "Yellow Circle Days." These were special days on the calendar. They would become my favorite days. In my letter to Tony on Day 92, I would finally tell him about my calendar – his calendar.

Thursday, October 18 Day 92

Tony,

How great it is to turn around, as I am sitting at my desk, look towards the wall, and see YOUR calendar with a "yellow circle" marked around Friday, October 19th! I just marked a circle around today's day, Thursday the 18th, as I do every day…usually as I walk into my office in the morning. And to see the circle around the 19th…sweet!

As I look at the calendar I remember very sadly designing a 6-month calendar on one of my computer programs just for keeping track of each day that you are away at OYCP. After printing out the calendar I "customized" it. My customization entailed marking the beginning and the end of The ChalleNGe. I then placed circles and filled the circles in with a yellow highlighter for those days we would have the opportunity to see you or have you at home for an extended stay. Those are my favorites. They are my "Yellow Circle Days." And thankfully I was able to cheat, just a little, and see you on a BONUS day on Wednesday the 10th. It's cheating, I know...but, what the heck!

So, tomorrow is "Yellow Circle Day;" a favorite day while you shape your life into a powerful new one...full of future success...full of excitement. I know there will be bumps in the road. There always are...but man, you have to be excited about what you have to look forward too! And tomorrow we get to see you!

After this "Yellow Circle Day" it will be just a bit more than 30 days before you will be able to spend Thanksgiving with us. Man....it truly will be a Thanksgiving. This year we certainly have something to be thankful for! And we will have a little over 5 days with you, and you with your friends too. Then 23 days until your graduation from the ChalleNGe! Ask me....do I count the days? Yep! Just like you!

I don't think you have seen, but around YOUR calendar on the wall I have a large picture I printed out of you on one knee and in your white tux and hat. I like that picture a lot. So do visitors to my office when I brag on you! That picture sits below the calendar. Above it I have another large 7x10 picture of you in your white tux with your "A's" cap on. To the right of that I have a picture I made just a week after you entered The ChalleNGe that was posted on the OYCP site and has you folding clothes (imagine that). Stuck on top of that picture, held by masking tape, is the postcard copy like I sent to you of your line-up and boys receiving their Pre-ChalleNGe Certificates, those many weeks ago.

Having the calendar and the pictures helps me each day. As I have said before, your 5-plus months at the ChalleNGe was never a thought as you were growing up. I had not planned on your extended stay away from home for half the summer before your senior year...and lasting until the mid-point of your senior year as well. It was just never a consideration, was it? I know that you too would have never scripted it this way if you would have been writing a book on your life as a senior in high school!

But here is how I look at it today. Thousands of kids across the United States leave their home, many in their senior year, to study abroad! You know, foreign exchange students and students who leave their senior year to attend foreign universities for one year. Well, this is much like that...except it is better...because we know you are just a few miles away and we have the opportunity to see you every so often!

This I know! You are learning more in this 5+ month program than you would ever learn at any high school or university in or outside of the United States! Do you realize that? Where could you have gone...that would have benefited you as much as the ChalleNGe? We are so lucky. You are so fortunate.

Nevertheless, it never was part of the plan. But, we have adapted. You too! And...I love "Yellow Circle Days!"

I love you

Your Dad

I lived for "Yellow Circle Days." I loved "Yellow Circle Days."

He was never far from my thoughts during his entire time away and dealing with his absence was never easy, especially at the very start.

Thankfully, his first weekend from home we were scheduled to travel to baseball games for Christiano in Portland, but driving to Portland without having Tony with us was strikingly apparent and even uncomfortable. Nici, who seldom missed a game wasn't able to make the trip with us and drove over in her car with our dog Copper. As we wound and wove through the mountains, much of the conversation touched on Tony. Even when we sat quietly, driving over the beautiful Cascade Mountain Range, we all knew that if we weren't saying anything, we were probably thinking of Tony. It was consuming, but still, we had to make sure Christiano knew his life was every bit as important as anything in our lives. I'm guessing much of his thinking as he was riding quietly in the back seat were of Tony and not focused strictly on the big game like most of his counterparts. If they lost this game they would surely drop to the losers' bracket of this three-day tournament.

Once we found the ballpark, which was always an adventure for us, we scouted for a position where we might keep dry. It seems like it always rains in Portland; but of course, it doesn't. We often sat behind center field for the games. I'm sure many of the parent's thought we felt we were too good to sit with them and all the other parents, who were usually huddled together in the same area somewhere around or behind our teams' dugout. That was never the case, really. We chose to sit away from parents for a couple of reasons. Leann and I, along with our kids, enjoyed this time as "our time." Maybe we enjoy "our time" together and with our kids to an extreme, but when we sat away from the others we didn't have to listen to or take part in negative conversations. You know the ones, right? "That damn coach, he doesn't know what he is doing," or "why doesn't he put my kid in the line-up?" Alright already!

Today was just a little different. I knew I would probably be peppered with questions about Tony's whereabouts since he always attended the games with us. So today, I wanted nothing more than to not have to answer questions of parents who were likely less concerned about Tony and more interested in his and our dilemma. I think there is a sick human instinct to find pleasure in discovering other people's troubles. Maybe it was just me.

I brought my journal with me should I feel the need to write and I did, for a while; but the raindrops kept smearing the ink and I finally placed my journal inside my coat, even though we had found some protection under the massive green center field scoreboard above our heads.

Christiano's team lost the game 4-2 on this first day of three and my thoughts of Tony were constant. As the team was gathering their equipment and meeting for an after-game session with the coaches to review the game, I stayed in my wet chair underneath the scoreboard. The rain had lessened a bit and Leann, Nici, and Copper walked over to the area where Christiano was packing his things into his baseball equipment bag, which always managed to take up most of the trunk of the car.

I pulled my journal out and wrote: "As you go about your day, know this…at many times during the day I am thinking of you…I mean…literally thinking about you. I hope you can feel it…you are not alone." I needed for Tony to know just how much he was loved and missed.

The weekend allowed plenty of time for writing and working "on" my business.

My own personal discovery of working "on" my business instead of merely working "in" it provided me with the opportunity to innovate, quantify, and orchestrate the direction my business follows. Isn't this exactly where I was headed with Tony? It was my hope all along to help inspire him and help him grow and my way of doing it was much the same as with my business. I think it is very true that few of us take time to work "on" our lives instead of just the things happening "in" our lives. The letters gave me pause to sit down and not just write letters, but to plan them. I found power in working "on" my letters to make absolutely certain they would provide Tony with everything he would need during The ChalleNGe. I broke it down into segments.

The first two-weeks of the ChalleNGe was called the Pre-ChalleNGe (I believe this phase is now called Red Stage). The first two weeks are brutal. I knew that Tony would need plenty of encouragement, especially during this period. So, I built my letters to focused on his likely being homesick, tired, sore, lonely, discouraged, overwhelmed, scared, and maybe a bit angry.

Even before Tony's first day at the OYCP I had written down *specific* ideas and thoughts that might empower him, especially the first two weeks. I remember writing notes in my journal outlining those topics or ideas so I could incorporate them into my letters. I would write my letters with a single theme and sometimes more, depending on my mood and the flow of the letters. For example, during the first two-week period, I wrote of and/or about the following:

- How Often I Think Of You
- Take One Step At A Time
- Never Lose Sight

- Build On Your Experiences
- You Are Exceptional
- Doing The Work To Accomplish Your Dreams
- Discover Who You Really Are
- The Will To Succeed
- Stand Up To Your Obstacles
- Second Chances
- One Reason Why You Can

I wanted to be certain I was on the same page with what he was learning and hearing from the cadre and the teachers at the OYCP and I wanted to know he was headed in the right direction and maybe most importantly, that he had not been forgotten, for even a minute, at home and that he was loved and valued. After all, isn't that we are all looking for in life?

It isn't any coincidence that many of these same specific ideas were those that I had used to train, motivate, and inspire agents working in and for my company. Most are really applicable in each of our lives, don't you think? Listen, we all deal with struggle. We all face fear in one way or another. We all fail, always hoping to fail forward; but that doesn't always happen either. I am reminded of something I heard one of my business coaches, Brendon Burchard, say. It went something like this, "you know humanity only has two recurring characters in its narrative and that's struggle and progress, most of us don't want the struggle, but if we throw out the struggle it is very likely we will never experience progress." Of course, struggle is part of life. My goal with Tony and with my real estate agents was to see progress and experience it's many benefits and realize the journey was worth it.

The second phase, called the Residential Phase (now known as White Stage) was the next 20-week period of the program at OYCP. During this period, there is still a focus on physical fitness, but a primary emphasis of placing the kids in the classroom takes hold. For Tony, I knew that I needed to support his efforts in the classroom by encouraging him to study hard and to complete his work to the best of his ability and on time. My letters to Tony provided "comfort food" to him, if you will.

The "comfort food" I provided focused only on the good news from home. Never did I talk about issues that might move his focus from the job ahead for him. I spoke of mundane and everyday events at home, but never concerning, for example, news of a friend being involved in a car accident or a relative who had fallen and broken her leg in three places. Nothing was included in the letters that would divert his focus. Remember, he hadn't been able to spend 90 minutes reading without leaving the classroom at Mountain View High School. So how on earth would he ever be able to sit quietly and attentively at OYCP? I recalled the test I was given of holding the book out in front of me or watching the young cadet on his hands and knees mopping up water with a sponge on the drill floor. How on earth would he ever manage?

The final phase is called the Post-Residential Phase. This phase is the "after" graduation period that partners the youth with their mentor in moving forward by returning to school, graduating from their high school, obtaining their GED, or finding a job. It is the period for keeping the kids on task and it is critical. I believed that if I didn't have an effective plan for my letters to Tony, what we would achieve would be purely accidental. I realized that on Monday, July 23rd, just four days after Tony had entered the Oregon Youth ChalleNGe.

12

THE PROSPECT OF SUCCESS

A journey of a thousand miles begins with a single step.

Lao Tzu

I drove to the neighborhood mailbox just a couple blocks from our house and there it was – the first letter. I couldn't open it quickly enough, but I called Leann at work so I could share it with her first as I didn't want to be alone. What would he say? I thought as I sat back in my car with the door closed and the air conditioner running full blast.

"Leann! I have a letter from Tony."

"What did it say? She questioned me with a raised voice.

"Well, I didn't want to read it without you. Do you have a minute? It is only a page long."

The letter was written on wide-lined notebook paper, the kind you purchase every fall as part of every school supply list in America. Much to my surprise, it was legible and easy to read. He had used a pencil. I wondered why he had written it with a pencil instead of a pen. The letter took less than a couple of minutes to read in its entirety. As I read it, I dissected each word as carefully as I dissected my first frog in Mr. Arndt's biology class in 1969.

"What do you think, Jim," Leann asked?

"Well, I don't think he hates us, so that is good," I answered back.

For the next few minutes I sat in the comfort of my car. I could see the heat roll off the hood through my windshield. I wager I read Tony's letter at least five or six times, each time trying to find another morsel of information that would give me a hint of what he was experiencing.

His first letter to me read, in part:

Hey, everything is all alright. I have accepted why I am here. It sucks. Sucks real bad. I don't sleep at night because I miss home so much and all I can think about is how good you guys have it. Dad, if you get a call from me saying I wanna quit, I'm sorry, but don't let me. I'm gonna do this. All I think about is you four. Mom, I love you and miss your cooking. Nici, I miss watching Dr. Phil with you. Yanno, I miss beating you up. I miss all that...but the end prize keeps me going. I will see you all very soon.

Much Love, Tony.

As I read his first letter I felt sadness. At that moment, I felt emptiness. *How selfish am I?* Here is a young man, whose longest time away from home had been a 4-day basketball camp at the University of Iowa when he was 12 and another basketball camp when he was 16 near Salem, Oregon. He knows this isn't about a few days, but almost 6 months!

Only someone who has actually climbed up to the mountaintop knows the preparation, the stamina, and the grit needed to make it. Tony's mountain was mighty tall. Mountain analogies are used all the time here in Bend, Oregon. After all, some of the Cascades highest peaks are just outside of our front door. He spoke of "the end prize" in his letter. We knew that, like the climbing of any mountain such as Mt. Everest or Mt. Hood or Mt. Bachelor, that his journey would be long and hard. *But this hard? Dear God, will he be able to climb this mountain?* I remembered reading that between the years 1920 and 1952 seven major expeditions tried and failed to make it to the top of Mount Everest. This is one expedition that could not fail.

* * *

When parents were gathered at orientation on March 24, 2007, we were explicitly told that there was a good possibility that our child might call home, especially within the first two-week period, asking to come home and for someone to pick them up. Mr. Frank Strupith told us that it was important to say NO should a candidate call asking to come home. "They may call crying, begging, pleading, and screaming to come home. You must be firm, parents," he said. "Surely, should you bend on this, they may never have another opportunity to complete high school and move in the right direction with their lives."

That happened the very next day after receiving Tony's first letter. Mail arrives at about 1:30pm every day. I must admit, I left work at 1:00 p.m. to position myself near the mailbox to see if any mail was placed in our slot. The mailman pulled up, like I would guess he does each day, opened the door and swung open the entire south side of the mailbox cabinet. I could see the slots from where I was parked. I'm guessing 50 slots were exposed and I could see some had mail from the day or days before. The box that I thought was ours was empty. He juggled the envelopes from one slot to another in no apparent order or system. I saw what I thought were several envelopes being placed in our slot. *Good lord, and, hurry up so I can see if there is a letter from Tony.* Finally, he swung the large metal door closed and placed his key in the key hole to lock it up. I'm sure if anyone was watching, they must have thought I was looking for a million-dollar check in the mail by the way I ran to the box with my mailbox key in hand. Well, if they thought that, it was almost as important. There it was, another letter from Tony. Jackpot! I hurried back to my car and once again grabbed my cell phone to call Leann.

"Leann, we've got another letter from Tony. Do you want me to open it and read it or would you rather we open it and read it together?"

I thought it was only right to share his letters together. Maybe I thought this would be best, perhaps so we could support each other with any bad news and celebrate together if he might have good news. We were, after all, in this together. Thankfully, she answered, and she was able to take a couple minutes and listen while I read:

Hello family!

Everything is great! I truly mean that. I can't believe I said it...but it's true. I slept for the first time last night (his third night there) and there is only 10 days and it's done (the two-week pre-ChalleNGe phase) and they say time flies there and you won't want to leave. How is Yanno? How did his weekend baseball tournament go? Dad, is business any better? I pray each night that you begin to start selling more homes. Mom, do you like your new spot they gave you at the bank? I bet it has a great view! How is Nici? In a little over 4 weeks we get our first break (Labor Day) and I get to come home. I'm stoked! Well, not much else to say. Days are getting shorter and I know it is gonna start flying in no time. It isn't too hard. It's hard, but not real bad. So, yeah, hope to hear from you soon. I miss you all so damn much but I am starting to feel like a man! I love you all...back to you soon!"

Love Tony

When Leann arrived home after work she wanted to hold the letter and read it for herself. She too, always looking for a message or notion she might have missed. What a relief, we both thought.

We hadn't been home for more than an hour or so when Nici pulled up, envelope in hand.

"Hey Nici," I exclaimed. "We got a letter from Tony today!"

She didn't seem to share the same enthusiasm I was demonstrating.

"Here, Nici. Read it," I said.

"Well, by the look on your face I am guessing he held back a little, dad," Nici stated.

"What do you mean?" I probed.

"Here," she said. "I'll read the letter you and mom received from Tony and you read mine."

I opened her slightly torn envelope, took a single written page out, unfolded it and began to read. My heart sank and what had been a great day changed in Tony's first sentence to her.

Hey Nic,

Wow, I'm balling right now. I am home sick as all hell. I've almost called dad a few times to come and get me. But hearing you say I can make it, and dad too, is what gets me to say, "Screw that, watch me get through this. I am gonna get that high school diploma. I love you so much. I will be home and graduated in no time. This is hard ass as hell...but I will make it. I will. So, that's all for now, See you in a few weeks for break. Ten more days...and they say it is nothing after that! I love you. Never Forget that!

Love, Tony

Tony and the candidates are allowed less than an hour every day to write letters home. Letter writing generally takes place after a long and difficult day of training when they go to their bunk area for the night. Many candidates are so tired that they fall asleep with pencil and paper in hand, from what Tony told me. Some candidates' arms are even too tired to write as a result of the number of push-ups, pull-ups, and physical requirements of the day. The OYCP understands the importance of letters. They get it. On this day, we had two letters, one to Leann and me and one to our daughter Nici, likely written within a few minutes apart from each other and each telling a quite different story.

You might think that Tony had a motive in mind. Perhaps, but I learned later that he knew his sister could handle the truth more than Leann and me. You know what I am talking about if you are a parent. I remember telling my brother and sister things I would never tell my parents. Sometimes to protect my hide and probable punishment from a very strict father, and of course, brothers and sisters always understand more than mom and dad ever would, right? I would come to know that Tony would protect us a bit in each of his letters to me and I guess I too was writing in a way to protect him.

Nevertheless, on this night, I lay awake imagining the hurt and the pain he was feeling and knowing that the only thing I could do...that I must do...is to allow him to experience the ChalleNGe. I realized that the pain a parent feels when their child is suffering doesn't end when they reach a certain age or a certain time. I could visualize the tears rolling down his face as I lay awake and stared at the dark ceiling in my bedroom, only lit by the light sneaking through a separation in the seam of our curtains. I could see him wipe his nose with a quick swipe of his right arm from his elbow to his wrist, from right to left, probably doing everything he could to hide his emotions from others. But then again, he wasn't alone. He wasn't the only one hurting.

I was trying to imagine how some kids were feeling who had not received a letter that day or any of the first few days from home. A young boy or girl who had never really known the dedicated and unconditional love of a parent. So, for now I knew he was safe and he was given plenty of time to think and to reflect on the reasons he was at the ChalleNGe. I remember, when attending orientation, Frank Stupith reassuring all of us that "this will be the hardest thing your son or daughter has likely ever experienced, but we will care for them. They will be safe. It is also likely this is the hardest experience you have gone through with your child as a parent. Know that we care."

A journey of a thousand miles begins and ends with one step."
LAO – TZU
Ancient Chinese Philosopher

My sixth letter sent to Tony on July 24th, crossed paths with one he had written to me and mailed just the day before. I hadn't read his letter before sending mine…but the timing for my letter of encouragement could not have come at a better time.

First, his letter sent to Leann and me. This letter was overwhelming for both of us. It wasn't what we wanted to hear from Tony. The letter was short, but packed full of so many emotions.

This letter was addressed to both Leann and me, but it was personalized to his mother.

Hey ma,

This sucks. All the work is easy and I'm physically fine, but I am so homesick…all I do is cry. I wanna come home so bad, I don't know what to do. I'm gonna make it thru the next week and I will see from there. I'm not going to continue if I'm unhappy. There is no point. I miss you so much. I love you mom. I'll be okay. Hopefully it gets better.

So that's all. It's going to be a long night. We have three hours of PT, so we will see. Love you mom. Never forget that I should be home in no time. Hopefully it moves fast. I miss your food mom. This food is alright, but nothing like yours.

Love you. Hugs and Kisses,

Tony

If this was just Day 5, how much worst might it get? Clearly, the ChalleNGe was breaking him down, and breaking him down I believed exactly as intended and designed. At least I thought that had to be the right thing.

Remember, there are kids at the ChalleNGe who, in their minds and in their world, are the baddest, meanest, roughest, and toughest around. Kids from homes where neglect and abuse are the norm. Young men and women who found acceptance only in street gangs or in coffee shops where they hung out with their friends instead of attending school. At the same time, there are gentle kids, troubled kids, kids who might not have been accepted by their peers, teachers, and even their family. Some who just were lost or unable to function in an often-failed educational model that teaches in a "one size fits all" environment, if in fact, some might argue, they teach at all. We know not everyone finds their way the same as others.

Still, I believe The ChalleNGe was setting these kids up for success thru what appeared to be unsurmountable odds. I mean, there was clearly nowhere else for Tony to go. It must have been the same for the majority of the 160 kids who wrote home from their bunks that night too. Perhaps, his admission in "I don't know what to do" or "if I'm unhappy there is no point" was his admission of almost complete surrender.

Coincidently, the letter I sent to Tony, on the same day I received his, was a letter that would strengthen him and prove his resolve. I could only hope so. I couldn't imagine getting the phone call asking to come home or the phone call from the cadre requesting that we come and pick him up. Remember, he can walk away anytime and kids do. As I read his letter I contemplated the fact that it would be so easy for Tony to walk out that door and head for home. I stopped for a minute and tried to calculate how long it would take for him to get home from The ChalleNGe should he decide to leave.

Let's see... When I was in boy scouts in 1967, we hiked from Camp Ingawanis through a densely wooded and hilly trail to what have must have been the Rock Island or Illinois Central railroad tracks that took us into the small northeastern Iowa town of Waverly, Iowa. I remember the hike almost like it was yesterday. I also remember our scoutmaster, Royce King, telling us it was about a five-mile hike. That hike took us 45 minutes. So, if our home is located 6 miles from the ChalleNGe it would take Tony probably an hour. He knows how quickly and how easy it would be to leave and be home in a matter of minutes, I thought. It wasn't like many of the other kids at the Oregon Youth ChalleNGe who had come from all areas of the State of Oregon, some six or seven hours away by car, not by foot!

Isn't it funny that while I was thinking of my hike and the time it would take him to get home after reading his letter, that in my letter, sent before reading his, referenced the quote, "A journey of a thousand miles begins and ends with one step." *Would he connect with my quote only a day after referencing the possibility of leaving if things didn't improve?*

My letter to him on day six was filled with news and events from home. I spoke about the baseball games from the weekend and I went on in this letter to talk about the local county fair, that I hadn't seen any of his friends, and that I had been on the OYCP Website.

I got onto the OYCP website today to see, if by some chance, there were any new pictures posted that might include you! There weren't any, so I guess I will have to wait 38 more days until I get to see your pretty face.

I touched on my business, too. On that morning, I had interviewed two real estate agents. In the first 90 days of opening, I was up to 14 licensed agents.

I interviewed two agents today...and I think both will come into my office! I think that will be 16, Tony. I am getting there...it is just a matter of how long I can endure this drought of a selling season.

I knew there was no going back. I had leveraged everything Leann and I had to purchase the Exit Realty International franchise. I mean everything! Like Tony, I was in a position where I had to be successful. I had to endure what I never expected. I, too, had to face adversity, so it was clear: we both had a lot in common with one-another. More than I had ever realized. Then I reflected on the quote and said:

Your journey began months ago, Tony. It began when you made the decision to apply for entrance in OYCP. And while this more than 150-day program, taking you away from home, might seem like a thousand miles... you have the right approach in knowing that it will go fast and yes...one step at a time.

I know you will be thinking of the one step at a time approach as you are marching and running at OYCP.

Then I tried to emphasize the life journey we had, at this point, taken together.

We have surely traveled a thousand miles together in your short life and it took us 18 years to get to where we are, again, one step at a time. Right? Your first day of school. Getting into the car when I picked you up from daycare at Vonna's house. The two of us going to basketball games and watching the Huskies at Oelwein High School play. And to having you and Michael Warsaw hit balls to me on the baseball field at Skyline Park while I staggered towards the ball (quit laughing, Tony). The journey will be hard and long. But we must move forward. Me in my business and you at the ChalleNGe we must. It is okay to look back from time to time. Looking back allows us to realize our mistakes.... but never lose sight of WHAT IS IN FRONT OF YOU!

I then drew out a VISION CHART for him to consider as he looked for those things ahead of him and in his future. Things that he and I knew would be possible only by completing the program.

It looked like this:

- Graduation
- Career
- Laughter
- Girlfriends
- Snowmobiling
- Travel
- Friends

The Prospect of Success

- Driving
- Love
- Family
- Job
- Lifelong Education
- Boats
- Fun

I had learned of using vision charts years ago. The practice incorporates the use of pictures to remind you of those things important to you in your life and those things you have on your list. All of us have photographs and souvenirs to remind us of important things that have happened in or that are part of our lives, right? My goal in business, for both myself and for my agents, is to keep a clear vision of what it is each of us wishes to achieve. Some people may jot down those things they wish to accomplish by keeping a "bucket list." The chart I have created in my business life and the one I created for Tony was to bring an *awareness* of what I thought might be important in his life. I knew, at least for these first two weeks of pre-ChalleNGe and certainly on only the seventh day of The ChalleNGe when he would receive my letter, that a reminder of why he was there would be appropriate and helpful.

I ended my letter by saying,

You are just preparing to connect the dots, Tony! You're doing great! What you are doing is fantastic! Mom and I are so proud of you. You know that, right?

One step at a time....

Love you!

I made a point of not sharing my pain at his being away with Tony. The program had advised us to keep all communication positive, so I didn't mention that I missed him so much that I just had to be near him even if I couldn't actually see him.

When you drive into the Oregon Youth ChalleNGe grounds, if you take notice, you will see what looks to be a winding trail throughout an area made up of mostly a light brownish combination of sand and dirt, sagebrush, and craggy ancient juniper trees. The soil in littered with rocks protruding out of the soil; some with sharp jagged edges and others rounded or flat. The trail, I was told, is an area where the attendees of the ChalleNGe run and perform some of their physical fitness training. Sometimes, living just six miles from the OYCP facility was a good thing. Other times it was almost haunting.

At times during my day I would look in that direction and speculate what I might see if I were positioned just across the road. I mean, I was so close I could easily take a drive out there and sit in waiting. Other parents didn't have that luxury; but, I did. Maybe if I did drive out to The ChalleNGe I might see Tony running on the outdoor trail or see him as he left in a facility vehicle to drive into town or maybe on their way back. Heck! I don't think there was a law preventing me to find a place to park my car and hang out there once and awhile. *Who would do that?* Sadly enough, I did. Especially the first two weeks.

If there was a time I could escape from work, I would. Sometimes I would just make the drive and slowly pass by the grounds at OYCP looking for signs of anything, other times I would drive, maybe a quarter of a mile up the road, turn around and do it again. I even found a driveway that had a view of the outdoor running trail; not the entire course, but enough to give me a glimpse of someone running by. I would sit sometimes for an hour, maybe longer. Most of the time I wrote in my journal or wrote letters to Tony.

I never mentioned in my letters that I often sat just yards from where he might be sitting or talking or studying or eating or carrying out his PT work. I never told Leann either. I didn't tell anyone, actually. I didn't want Leann to think I was some pathetic, sad, and hopeless father. I didn't want for her to see any more weakness from me than she had already witnessed in me these past months. I mean, the challenges my failing business was facing, along with the circumstances of Tony's situation had already shown I might not be that steady, confident, and talented man she thought she had been married to for the past 27 years.

Everything was exposed here. My sitting on the side of the road and my driving slowly back and forth in front of The ChalleNGe facility and my journal and letter writing was my personal moment of frailty and weakness, of looking for strength and direction. For me. For Tony. For the licensed real estate agents in my offices.

I recall driving to "my driveway" on day nine. It was another warm, no, hot Friday. We were headed into the second weekend without Tony and his stay at The ChalleNGe. I took my journal with me. I had started a letter and thought perhaps I would finish it and get it mailed before 5:00 p.m. so Tony might receive it as early as tomorrow.

There isn't very much traffic on Dodds Road, but every few minutes a car might drive past. Each driver and passenger looking my way, probably wondering why I was sitting there with my windows down and backed into a driveway or more likely thinking I was a cop running radar. Funny, my car always caught the eye of passersby; not because it was stunningly beautiful or unique, but because it was a white 2000 Mercury Marquis, the same body style of most police and state trooper cars at that time. I would often get a chuckle from people whom I knew were slowing down because they thought I was a cop in an unmarked patrol car.

It was quiet there, at least until a large truck or tractor would pass by. Busy Highway 20 is about a quarter of a mile down the road, so the loud semis and excessively obnoxious motorcycles were within earshot. I could see planes, mainly small single engine planes, pass above me coming and going from the nearby airport; but, generally, it was quiet which gave me plenty of time to think. Mostly I thought about the fact that things didn't seem to be going as well as I had hoped.

13
"DAD, I'M GOING TO SUCCEED"

Physical fitness is not only one of the most important keys to a healthy body, it is the basis of dynamic and creative intellectual activity.

John F. Kennedy

Luckily things turned around thanks in large measure to Tony's physical prowess, something that not all the kids in the program possessed.

They came in all sizes. Tall. Short. Slender. Overweight. Both boys and girls. You would swear some of the candidates had never seen a gymnasium. And honestly, I think most of the candidates had found other interests rather than body-building, jogging or…well…walking. So, when I looked over the incoming candidates that first day of The ChalleNGe I scratched my head questioning the ability of some of these kids being able to get through that first two weeks, let alone the grueling five-and-a-half months.

Through it all, I never, for a moment, worried about Tony being able to withstand the physicality of the program, and thankfully, he made his way through the toughest physical training he had ever endured. Now, this kid had seen some tough physical training with his high school football and basketball teams. The head basketball coach at Mountain View, Craig Reid, had his kids running all the time. I often stopped by Tony's basketball practices and witnessed the constant running and wind sprints he and the other members of the Cougar team were put through; so, heck, if he could withstand Coach Reid's practices, he would surely do well at the ChalleNGe.

Before the end of Pre-ChalleNGe, each candidate is given the opportunity to take part in the President's Physical Fitness Test. Actually, it probably would be better said that every candidate is required to take the President's Physical Fitness Test. Man, I remember taking the test each year when I was in junior high school. I wasn't excited about taking the test way back then in the 60's and my being a fat kid always made it significantly harder.

As I looked at the calendar parents had been given on the first day at intake, I could see that the end of Pre-ChalleNGe was on Friday, August 3rd. I knew this was a pivotal date. If he could get through the first two weeks surely, he could get through the remainder of the ChalleNGe.

Trouble is, I wouldn't know if he had successfully made it to the next stage until receiving a letter from him some time after the Pre-ChalleNGe Ceremony where candidates receive their completion certificates, name tag, and the honor of moving from candidates to cadets. There are no phone calls. No texts. No emails. Leann and I, like the other parents would need to wait for a letter.

I went through the weekend not knowing if he had made it to the next step, but I hadn't received a call from Tony saying, "Pick me up Dad…I'm outta' here." When the phone rang, I wasn't sure I even wanted to answer it. What would I do if he had not successfully completed the first stage of the ChalleNGe? What would I say if it were he calling me?

On Monday, I went to my familiar position by the mailbox on the corner of Oakview and Larkview Road. Before I could do that, however, I had a sales meeting for the agents at my office. So, it was about 1:00 p.m. before I could make my way towards the mailbox near my home. I was a bit perturbed that a previously scheduled sales meeting with my real estate agents would delay my retrieving Tony's letter. More upsetting was that only 3 of my 8 agents showed up.

Finally, I made it to the mailbox. *There had to be a letter from Tony.* I walked from my car to the mailbox, opened it and no letter, in fact, no mail was in our slot at all. That is a good sign, I assured myself. If there isn't any mail it must be that the mailman hasn't made his stop at our neighborhood mailbox yet. I climbed back in my car, looking up and down the street to see if perhaps the mail delivery vehicle might come in my line of sight. Nothing. I drove several blocks from my mailbox to another cluster of boxes to see if the mail delivery vehicle was there. Nothing. As I was driving I received a call. I looked at the caller ID and saw it was Leann calling.

"Hey, have you had time to check the mail?" she asked.

"Yes, and nothing from Tony!" I said with a huff that I am sure reflected my disappointment. "I'm hoping the mailman is a little late today," I added.

I heard her sigh on the other end. She, too, was feeling the frustration of not knowing and I guess hearing a sigh of relief or a sigh of frustration is pretty normal in the course of things, right? But her breath on the other end seemed different this time. I don't know.

"Listen," I said. "I will check the mailbox in a few minutes and call you when I get the mail. I'm sure there is a letter in the box from Tony."

"Okay. Thanks. Talk to you soon," she said before hanging up.

It was one of those moments where nothing more needed to be said. I know how she felt, but I recall thinking about Leann and how much was never said between us about Tony going to the ChalleNGe. Yes, we talked, but I don't think, to this day, that I have ever asked her to tell me how hurt she was when she saw Tony turn and walk through the door entering the ChalleNGe. *Jesus Christ help me! How selfish am I, anyhow?* I don't recall reaching out to her the way I should have. I don't remember offering my shoulder for her. I don't remember lovingly putting my arms around her to absorb some of the pain she felt even though I knew she was in agony. I don't recall wiping the tears from her eyes that surely ran down her cheek countless times as we lay in bed before falling asleep after another long day without Tony.

Clearly, I was too absorbed in my own self-pity to reach out to offer my hand to her. But there is no excuse for my acting like I didn't notice the hurt she was feeling. If I could, I would change that. I hope she doesn't, somewhere deep down, hold some bottled-up anger or disappointment for how I wasn't there the way she might have hoped I would be or expected me to be. How does one act when their son or daughter is sent away from home for nearly six months in their senior year of high school, anyway? I guess this is as good of place as any to apologize to her if she ever felt I wasn't there for her.

I decided to just go home and wait a while and try again in maybe 30 minutes or so. It was Friday and during the summer months in Bend real estate agents find any excuse to leave work early for the weekend. My agents had already indicated that they had more important things on their mind. So, I felt maybe I would just take the rest of the day off at this point. It was already 1:30. I would have thought the mail carriers would have the same idea, you know, to get their work done and home for the weekend; but I guess they don't have the same luxury of cutting out for the day when there is mail to be delivered. Heck, maybe Friday is a heavy mail day?

I walked in the house and greeted our dog, Copper, with a pat on the head and took my place known as the Big Green Chair. I hadn't been there more than ten minutes before Nici called.

"Hey dad! Any word from Tony?" she asked.

"Notta, but I am home. I just went to the mailbox and I am home for the day. So, I'll be checking the mail here in a half hour or so." I replied.

"Okay, well, text me if you get a letter from him." she concluded.

"You do the same," I said before hanging up.

"I struck GOLD," I said to Leann as I walked away from the mailbox about a half hour later with a letter in one hand from Tony and my cell phone in another.

"Well, did he make it." she asked.

I answered back, "I don't know, Leann, I haven't opened up the letter yet because there are six of them here!"

"What?" she exclaimed.

"Yea, so that explains the dry spell with no letters. Give me just a second."

I made my way to the car and tore each envelope open, one at a time. They were all postmarked the same day, so I just looked at the first line or two for the letter that might give us the news we were looking for. Like so many of Tony's letters, it was just one-page long. The first sentence gave it all away!

"You ready, Leann?" I asked.

"Jim!" she replied in an almost hostile voice.

Dear Dad,

Well, today I did it. I got in my Class A Uniform and I had my name called and was presented with: a certificate, dog tags and a name tag. I DID IT! I GRADUATED FROM PRE-CHALLENGE!

I didn't get CPL (Cadet Platoon Leader) or team or squad leader.... but I received KP Leader Kitchen Patrol! That's right dad, I got a leadership off the bat. I'm stoked! Mr. Demarr chose me himself.

I'm gonna do it! Twenty more weeks' dad, and it's over! It's been hard, but know the hardest part is over. They say it's all downhill from here.

The days seem to get shorter and we get more time to just screw around at night.

I love you,

Tony

"Thank goodness," Leann said.
"Well, Leann, let's hope that he continues to "get it," I replied.

I returned home to read all six letters, but especially the letter telling us he had graduated from pre-ChalleNGe. I was alone, with the exception of Copper, and sitting in my green chair. I sobbed. I was so relieved. I was so happy for Tony. I was so thankful to God. Finally, He had looked down upon Tony and blessed him.

God hadn't forgotten.

* * *

I read a wonderful book by Art E. Burg, entitled *Some Miracles Take Time*. I think of it often as I go about my everyday business in real estate. In his book, he outlines how he overcame a tragic accident that had left him a quadriplegic. Thrown from a car, he had broken his neck and was paralyzed from the chest down. His doctors told him he would literally need to dream new dreams. He was told he would need to embrace new dreams accepting his limitations. He remembers his mother, however, saying to him, "Art, while the difficult takes time, the impossible just takes a little longer." He believed her and became the president of his own company and traveled far and wide telling others that "the impossible just takes a little longer." While Tony's story is quite a different story and not nearly as dismal and devastating as that experienced by Art, I had hoped I had learned something from his story and his quote that "the impossible just seems to take a little longer."

When Tony wrote this letter on August 3rd, 2007, it was the first time, in as long as I could remember, that he started something and successfully completed it. It must have been a huge relief and a euphoric experience for him. A kid who had lost the opportunity to compete in sports, the one area where he had experienced success in his life. A kid who was ignored, maligned, and mostly dismissed as a lost cause by many of his teachers, counselors, and coaches had, on this day, finally accomplished something that he could be proud of. For now, at least, all dissenting voices from the past were muted. I can't imagine the feeling. I, like you perhaps, have failed along the way at one time or another; but, for this kid it had been one continuous failure after another.

The next day was a fantastic day.

* * *

I had sent a note to Tony's Cadre, Mr. Demarr a few weeks after intake day. I had expressed a concern with Mr. Demarr about the possibility of coming face to face with Tony during OYCP'S programs that take them to a number of venue's around Bend. For example, you often find OYCP Cadets at parades, community events, and in situations where volunteers are needed. What would I do if I might attend an event where I came face to face with Tony? Am I allowed to say hello, smile at him, or even approach him and hug him, I wondered?

Phone calls to your child, while he or she is going through the program, are not allowed, unless, of course there might be an emergency situation; but on one particular day Mr. Demarr had made an exception.

I answered my phone to the voice of Cadre Demarr. "Good morning Mr. Mazziotti. I am calling today to answer your question about our procedures should you come face to face with your son, Tony, at an event where he and OYCP is participating." He explained the procedures clearly. Then, unexpectedly he said, "Mr. Mazziotti, I am sitting right here with your son, Tony. Would you like to say hello to him?"

My heart soared. My eyes filled with tears. At that moment, nothing else mattered.

"Well, of course I would Mr. Demarr," I exclaimed. Then, the next thing I heard, "Hi Dad!"

I was stunned. I wasn't expecting this call. Dammit, I thought! I wish Leann was here. She is going to be so disappointed.

"Tony, it is so good to hear your voice! Congratulations on completing the Pre-ChalleNGe. We are all so proud of you. Never prouder!"

"Thanks Dad, I appreciate it," he said.

I didn't know what to say next. Seldom at loss for words, I wanted to talk and just hold on to his voice for as long as I could.

"Things are good, Dad. I am doing well, was given a leadership position and I am going to succeed."

Exactly the words I'd been hoping to hear.

Then, as quickly as the call began, he said, "Well, Mr. Demarr just wanted to give me the opportunity to say hello. I've gotta run, Dad. Thanks for the letters. Tell Mom and everyone that I love them. Bye."

It was that quick, but it was fabulous. I'll never forget the feeling that overcame me. Certainly, one of the tiny moments that I so relish in my life.

14

GOING FOR IMPACT

Although it may seem hidden…when you search for your gift with an open mind and a free spirit, it will be there. Once you have found it, and you follow it with forage and persistence, it will reward you with happiness and deep satisfaction that nothing else can provide.

Lou Tice
The Pacific Institute

Tony had begun to figure out how to adapt to the ChalleNGe. His friends, their parents, and our family often asked me what the program was like for Tony during that time. I usually shared pieces of this letter with them to help provide them with some perspective of what "a day in the life" of Tony was like:

Pop,

Eh! Today, has been slow and I got in the weight room last night and just wrecked my arms. I couldn't even move this morning waking up! So, I have just been really off and slow all day. It's about 12:45 p.m. and I am done with school for the day because I have kitchen duty, which means I and two other cadets have to cook dinner.

So, we're in the kitchen from 1pm to 5 p.m. The cooks are really nice. They even turn on music and we get to relax and hang.

It was great getting your letters and news articles. All the boys say I have the best dad. I just say yeah, he's okay.... ha-ha!

Not much new besides school, school.

Time to go. I am sure we will get a lot of time to write tonight because we didn't have much allowed last night.

There was no time to write because we had to "celebrate" birthdays. Celebrate means that my cadre, Mr. Damarr, has those celebrating a birthday to do pushups while we sing happy birthday. It's all done in fun.

Got your letters, however. I will write tomorrow. Love you pop!

Tony

Now that Tony had completed what some say is the most difficult part of the ChalleNGe and accepted his new reality, it was time for me to help him discover the man I knew he could be. I had decided, even before writing to Tony at The Oregon Youth ChalleNGe, that "bullet pointing" my way to Tony's mind might be helpful to him, and perhaps all young students. I often remind the agents who work with and for me in my real estate office that without a destination there is no sure place to land. Likewise, once a destination is decided upon, it is helpful to have a roadmap to get there. Right? So, on a separate piece of paper, enclosed with a letter of August 16, I included one of the best road maps for life that I have seen.

"The Ten Choices You Will Regret In 10 Years" is something I tore out of a magazine article years ago and placed inside the pages of a book. I have seen variations of one sort or another of the "Ten Choices" and I have no idea who deserves the credit for writing it, but like many articles of this type, no single author probably is responsible for it. Often, these kinds of written pieces take on a life of their own. So, I created my "Ten Choices" based on what I was hoping Tony would take from the ChalleNGe and make it part of his life, well, forever.

THE TEN CHOICES YOU WILL REGRET IN 10 YEARS

1. Not Being True To Who You Are
2. Being Selfish and Concerned About Only You
3. Avoiding The Opportunity To Change, Grow, and Improve
4. Waiting Until Tomorrow To Move Forward
5. Accepting Less Than What You Deserve
6. Trying To Control Everything In The World
7. Associating With Those Who Breathe Negativity
8. Allowing Others To Create Dreams For You
9. Giving Up When Things Get Tough
10. Allowing Laziness To Stop You

These 10 Choices, in one form or another, were the basis of each letter I wrote. Oddly enough, many were the same ten that I had adopted in my life and worked to instill in my real estate team every day.

A perfect example might be my letter to Tony on August 1, day 14 of the ChalleNGe. In this letter, I built on a word I had read somewhere and I used pieces from another's words. I wanted to focus on how the ChalleNGe might serve as an excellent conduit for his achieving a "Great Life." The inspiration for this came from #5: Accepting Less Than You Deserve. I also included my own failed life issues to demonstrate that he wasn't alone and that I struggle every single day with being the best that I can be with the abilities I have. I worked with two important words in this letter; "Obstacle" and "Great Life."

For a long time, it seemed to me that a great life was about to begin, but there was always some obstacle in the way. Something had to be taken of first. There was always some unfinished business like bad coaches, certain friends, poor teachers, strict parents, rotten grades in school, girlfriends....and the list goes on.

I knew that if I could deal with these obstacles that it was then, and only then, when life would begin. At last....it dawned on me that obstacles were my life.

It's true Tony! We all have obstacles. I certainly do. For me it is being overweight, not always thinking things through before speaking, my temper, not telling your mom that I love her each and every day....and the list goes on and on. So, the key for me...and the key for you is to remove these obstacles so we can both have a great life!

So, why did I write this paragraph on "obstacles?" I did it Tony, because YOU, yes YOU...are in a place where you have the opportunity to begin removing obstacles from your life that have held you back. You have the opportunity to discover who you really are. You are now in a place and a time where you will find out why you have had unfinished business, maybe for years. You are and will discover why obstacles cannot and will not hold you back any longer. It is your time, Tony. It is only when you and I decide to face your life directly in the face that you and I will have the opportunity for a great life.

As I wrote the words I couldn't help but examine my own setbacks and the setbacks of those who were part of my real estate office. I often worked, and continue to work, with each of my agents to define their obstacles so they, too, won't ever be required to accept less than they deserve. Isn't it the same for all of us? We all have obstacles, don't we? For Tony, this was the time for him to plan for the future that was his for the taking and it was his to develop for a great life!

YOU HAVE TO ASK YOURSELF, WHO AM I? AND WHAT IS MY PURPOSE?

Early in September, around day 30, I felt that Tony was losing momentum, the "Big Mo," so to speak. Maybe he was comfortably settling in. We all do, don't we? I know this wasn't the OYCP's first rodeo. Their formula has yielded significant successes, but we had, by this time, about three plus months remaining to turn this kid around or possibly lose him. I know many other parents felt the same way. In fact, some parents were already losing their kids, as explained in Tony's letter to me on Tuesday, September 8, 2007. It read, in part:

Since we have been back from break (returned back on September 4th - Week 7) we have lost 4 cadets. The one whom you saw, one that failed to come back at all, one who just wanted out and left and one cadet who was sent home for hitting another cadet. So now we are down to 47 male cadets. We have the halfway part in just 10 days. We get to watch a movie and just kick back and chill. That should be fun. Other than that, not much is new here. Joe Padilla (his mentor) comes this Saturday! I am really looking forward to that.

More tomorrow.

Love you,

Tony

The ChalleNGe sometimes mirrored my own business where I work with adults. They, too, lose momentum and I constantly work to provide them with all the encouragement and the training I have, and then some. I also find myself losing momentum when everything doesn't go right and honestly, little was going right for me.

Traditionally, in real estate, the wind-down to the busiest season of the year is Labor Day and as the market slows, so do agents. This is a time where agents who have nothing in their book of business realize that the time is up; maybe, just like the two boys at OYCP who walked away from opportunity: one who decided it might be easier to get stoned rather than face his challenges; and another who found fighting might solve his problems.

Like a shot in the arm for Tony, his mentor, Joe Padilla, was scheduled to arrive at perhaps just the right time to re-energize Tony and dish up some optimism. Maybe just in the nick of time; and I knew that I didn't want him to follow those who were no longer cadets at the school of last chances. So, upon receiving the letter I took pen to paper:

Remember, Tony. You lost 4 cadets since the break, right? And remember that just 10 days ago, you said to me that you were "stoked." You were and are excited that maybe for the very time you are experiencing success and living with purpose!

Anyway, maybe I am making too much of your Tuesday letter and reading things that don't exist. But don't follow in the footsteps of the 4 boys that are now gone.

You cannot allow yourself to be mediocre any longer.

You are far more than ordinary. You are! You are exceptional. I have told you that many times over the years and it is just now you are discovering who you really are!

You know that every Friday morning I have an 8am meeting with all my agents. Each Friday we address their business and tomorrow I will be talking to them, as I am to you today about PURPOSE!

Remember, these are adults, Tony. I have 15 people and here is what I know. Only two people have PURPOSE. I try to motivate them. I have given them excellent tools but without purpose they accomplish little. It is like they are committing slow-motion suicide.

So, let me try this out on you 'because here is what I am going to ask them. Ready?

1. *Do you feel like you are running in place and not going anywhere?*

2. Do you have low expectations for the future?
3. Do you have low self-esteem and self-confidence?
4. Do you have clear goals?
5. Do you focus on being successful or ordinary?

I already know their answers. I can see it every day in them. But here is what is different about you. Think about it. You have stepped up to the plate. You have faced the music. Sure, mom and I helped move you along, but the choice to face this was all yours!

I believe your purpose right now is to demonstrate to yourself that you are the exceptional young man I see!

It is time to prove it to yourself!

You have to ask yourself: who am I and what is my PURPOSE?

I am convinced that when you leave OYCP as a graduate on December 19th, that you are going to be the same Tony in many ways. You are going to be the life of the party and the same great kid you have always been, kind, funny, and loving. But know you are going to have a new sense of PURPOSE! You have to Tony. You just must!

We love you and think about you 24/7,

DAD

I tried to make my letters as impactful as I could with the words that I would write each day, always. I also had decided to make my letters very visual and informational with news of the day that I knew he was missing. Let's face it, we have children who are connected to instant news and information at their fingertips from their laptops and their smartphones. I understood clearly that the ChalleNGe was acting as a mind detox facility for many of these kids. The method of placing troubled kids in a 100% controlled facility did just that. Removing the poison of drugs and alcohol for some. Replacing the friendship of gang members with the support of the cadre and fellow cadets. Removing the sometimes-mind-numbing video games, television, and YouTube videos, all of which are in full living color. Providing a safe environment away from an unstable and even dangerous family situation at home.

My goal was, even for just a few minutes, to provide Tony with things I knew he loved and enjoyed. My letters were often jammed packed full of newspaper clippings of up-to-the-moment sports results including NASCAR standings. Tony loved NASCAR. My principal real estate broker back in Iowa, Jim Hughes, had been considerate enough to bring Tony a program from the 2000 Daytona 500. It probably didn't hurt that we had spent time attending stock car races in Iowa just a few miles from our home. Heck, my real estate company even sponsored a car that raced every Saturday night in Independence, Iowa. I thought my kids would get a kick out of it as they saw "their dad's car" rounding the track; and, of course, I was hoping for some business from the investment in the paint job on the car. We attended many Saturday night races at the 3/8-mile dirt track sucking down soda, eating popcorn, and bringing home a mouthful of dirt flung on us by the cars as they spun, often sideways, around the dusty, dirt track.

I managed to include sports stories about the upcoming high school football season, some featuring his classmates and their comments. I wasn't sure how he would digest reading about what he was missing at his school. Would it upset him that he had put himself in a situation where he was missing the best year of his life? Or would he look at everything in a way that he might realize that "this" was in fact the best way to spend his senior year in high school. Would he realize that this was about much more than five months of his life? Would he get that this would be the springboard that gave him new hope, opportunity, and abundant encouragement?

My formula was to talk about home and mostly the common, and often boring, uneventful days we shared as a family. I would try to paint a visual picture for Tony with my words describing how Christiano had left for a one week trip with his favorite coach of all time, Coach Roberts, his wife Lori, and fellow classmate Trevor, to Coer'de Lane, Idaho. I talked about how I had hoped to go to a local grill to grab a burger with Leann, but that she had fallen asleep in her chair and really didn't want to leave the house anyway. I told him I had missed receiving letters from him on Friday and Saturday. I described to him the details of a car crash on the Indy Car Racing circuit and included a still photo of the crash. I wrote about the Sunday race as it was happening at Watkins Glen. I touched on his being homesick, asking if he was doing better and recounted homesickness I had felt when I had left home for college.

How is your homesickness Tony? Are you doing better? When I went off to college in 1972 I was homesick for a very long time.... actually, I couldn't wait to get home every weekend that I could. I really enjoyed being around my mom and dad, and my girlfriend from high school was still living back home. She stayed back and worked as she decided what to do with her life.

Thirty-eight laps to go at Watkins Glen, Tony! The caution flag is up and its Jeff Gordon in the lead.

Then I included a copy of the coming week's weather forecast. I thought he might want to know in the event they had outdoor activities scheduled for the cadets. I attached cartoons I thought he might enjoy and to put a smile on his face. For me, I would visualize Tony reading my letter and smiling, laughing, contemplating, and perhaps even crying.

Tony was a huge fan of Drew Carey, so I thought he should know that Drew Carey had suffered an arm injury while rehearsing on the set of The Price Is Right. I know he had to smile when I wrote:

Drew Carey got his arm caught in a moving part of a Price is Right grocery game and had to be taken to Cedars Sinai Hospital.

Okay.... two laps to go! Jeff Gordon was in first place and spun out on curve #1...ha! And the winner is Team Chevy...Tony Stewart! Hamlin finished second. It was a great finish. I wish you could have been here to see it.... but there will be many races in your lifetime.

I wrote about and inserted a photograph of the bus that had earlier fallen in the Mississippi River, not too far from our old hometown and where eight people had died as of my letter. I then wrote about how I believed writing in a journal and writing affirmations might help him. During this time, my company was learning from one of the great minds in the real estate world, Bill Nasby. Bill was a figurehead and trainer for the EXIT Realty Corp. International and I had learned greatly from him. He told me, "Self-image reinforcement is the key ingredient to all achievement and when you understand this law you can have anything you want.

I said to Tony:

How is your journal coming and what do you write in your journal, Tony? Is this something you will have the opportunity to keep? Might I make a suggestion? Now, I offer this suggestion only if you are allowed to write whatever you want in your journal. Try writing 15 affirmations each day. Your affirmations may be writing the same thing each day. The point of affirmations is that writing each day plants positive thoughts in your mind. Here are some affirmations I might suggest:

1. *I am powerful*
2. *I can achieve anything I chose to achieve*
3. *I awaken each morning anticipating a great day*
4. *I expect to be successful in everything I do*
5. *I know exactly what to do and I accomplish every goal I set*
6. *I excel in my studies*
7. *I easily find solutions to my problems*
8. *I am capable to complete every task*
9. *When I breathe I inhale confidence and exhale power*
10. *I live in the present and am planning for a fantastic future*
11. *I sleep comfortably and am fully rested when I awake*
12. *Nothing can stop me.*
13. *I attract positive people in my life*
14. *I have self-confidence and thrive*
15. *I love change and enthusiastically adapt to everything*

I completed this letter, like I completed so many of the letters I wrote to Tony, with words making sure he understood how much we love him and how proud we are of him.

Well, tomorrow it's back to work. I hope my agents have a good week and produce some sales. The weeks are going by so quickly and we are accepting the time you are away.

Sometimes it seems like you have been gone for months, but we are so content in knowing that things are going well for you. The short phone conversation we had last week helped and getting eight letters was great. We even saw you on the OYCP website, so trust me, that was a good week for us, Tony.

Mom also sends her best tonight. We sit and talk about you many times a day, always wondering what you are up to at that moment we are thinking of you. Let's see, it is almost 10 o'clock and I bet you are up in your bunk. Gosh! I haven't asked. Are you in the top bunk or lower bunk?

Hope you enjoy some of the stuff in this letter. It takes a while to put it all together, but it is worth it if you enjoy it. Maybe your buddies enjoy knowing what is happening too.

I'll write again tomorrow, Tony. Be safe. Be dedicated to reaching your goal. Be respectful to your superiors! Be attentive to your teachers. Keep a smile on your face.

Love you.

Dad

I don't know, I would guess this letter took a few hours writing on my computer, inserting photographs, and including charts; but it is all worth it when at the end of his letters I read,

I love you Dad! Thank you for everything you do for me. I miss you.

Love,

Tony

15
TONY'S FIRST VISIT HOME

Growth in love comes from a place of absence, where the imagination is left to its' own devices and creates you to be much more than reality would ever allow.

Coco J. Ginger

Home wasn't a set house, or a single town on a map. It was wherever the people who loved you were, whenever you were together. Not a place, but a moment, and then another, building on each other like bricks to create a solid shelter that you take with you for your entire life, wherever you may go.

Sarah Dessen
What Happened to Goodbye

Before we knew it, we were making plans for his first visit home. The Commandant for OYCP had addressed parents for a brief time when the candidates were receiving instructions in another room during Orientation. "Parents, start thinking about your plans for your first break with your son or daughters. First break is just six weeks away. This six-week period will be long and hard for the candidates. The six weeks will seem like an eternity for you as well. Please make that first break, six weeks from now, as special as you can. You will have just 4 days, a long Labor Day weekend to spend with your child. So, in your letters don't forget to give them something special to look forward to as a reward for a job well done should your son or daughter make it to that point. We believe it gives them the strength in making that extra effort that may be needed when things get tough here."

In the back of my journal I had collected some short stories and quotes I thought might inspire me when writing to Tony. I looked to the back of my journal where several pieces of paper dropped into my lap and down on the floorboard at my feet. As I picked them up, I quickly skimmed to see if anything grabbed my attention that might provide writing inspiration and direction. On one wrinkled piece of paper I had written:

If you will call your troubles experiences, and remember that every experience develops some latent force within you, you will grow vigorous and happy, however adverse your circumstances may be.

John Heywood

The words of John Heywood, a 13th century English playwright, seemed appropriate. My letters would find a way to center around, so to speak, the wisdom of others and I wrote the letters to expound upon their "experiences," or "the ability to build a latent force" and that by doing so "will help him experience happiness." I wondered if this might be too abstract for Tony. Nevertheless, I wrote. I didn't know any other way.

Exactly as the Commandant had suggested, I began with this letter to offer a reward that was within reach, just six weeks away. I thought of things we had postponed doing for years which I knew Tony and our entire family would enjoy.

Tony had spoken often about friends who had rented dune buggies on the southern Oregon coast and others who had experienced the hydro-boats weaving about on the Rogue River and even a quiet day enjoying the sunshine on a pontoon boat at a local lake. I wanted to make this a fabulous break for him and our family exactly as our trip to the Cove had been just 24 days before Tony would make his way to The ChalleNGe.

* * *

I honked the horn three times. One was always more than enough as far as Leann was concerned; but I swear, she never heard the first several honks. *For heaven's sake, it was time! Come on Leann.* I impatiently thought to myself. It's not like she wasn't as anxious as me. She is always up before me and in the shower before me. It's just how it goes around our house. *For heaven's sake…what is the hold up?*

I caught myself wanting to honk a few more times, but knew I had better not. She gets so angry when I do and that is half the fun. I kept quiet. Instead, I played around with the radio trying to find a station that Tony might like to listen to when he got in the car. I could see on the dimly lit display on my radio that it was 7:29 a.m. Today and this weekend was all about him.

I backed up my car just enough so I could see in thru the living room window from where I was parked in front of the house. I bent forward and backward to see if I could determine what Leann might be doing to cause the delay. I backed up just a bit more and I saw her bent over letting the dog in from an apparent bathroom visitation out the back-patio door. Heck, I had forgotten about the dog, usually my job to handle before we left the house.

I cracked the window on the passenger side of the car, the window closest to the house and could hear Leann praising

Copper on a "job well done." It was late enough in August where it might be getting cool enough to leave the front windows of our house closed, but not today. It was plenty warm and the front windows were wide open. "Good boy, Copper," I heard her say. "Is Tony coming home? Is he? Is he, Copper?" she said several times. Finally, she turned towards the front door of our house, locked it, and got in the car.

"Do you have everything, Jim?" she asked.

Thankfully she didn't mention my horn honking. *My God. It's like we are making final preparations as we leave for a two-week vacation.* Well, we weren't, but I would wager more time was spend planning this day and the upcoming Labor Day weekend than most family getaways.

This would be our first "official" visit to the ChalleNGe since leaving Tony there on July 19th. Our letters had kept us close, but not close enough. I was nervous. My stomach was a bit unsettled and I noticed the palms of my hands, usually cool and dry to the touch, were warm and damp. As I moved them across the fake woodgrain on my steering wheel, they would squeak. Leann was as nervous and as anxious as me.

"Do you think he will be happy to see us, Leann?" I questioned.

"Of course, Jim. Relax a bit, will ya?" she exclaimed.

Let's face it. Mothers know. They just know. So, as uneasy as I felt, I would go on her word.

We arrived at the long driveway leading to the ChalleNGe at about 7:45 a.m. It was only Leann and me. The special instructions we had been given stated that only parents or guardians were to report for the pick-up of their cadet. I had promised Tony we would be the first ones there, but there was already a line of about 12 or 13 cars at the gate. Each car was asked to stop at the entrance area secured by a tall chain link fence and a sliding gate and each met by a young man wearing a florescent vest over a tucked in green t-shirt. *Dammit! what if he is standing there waiting for us? We aren't going to be the first one's there and I promised him. Is he going to think we aren't excited as we have let on to be?*

When we finally got to the entrance gate we were welcomed by the young cadet.

"Good morning, sir. Welcome to the Oregon Youth ChalleNGe," he said with confidence. "Please follow the cars to the event parking area. Please proceed in to the facility through the large open door and someone will guide you through the procedure to pick up your son or daughter today," he concluded.

"Thank you, sir," I replied back, and we proceeded.

The parking area was perhaps 250 feet from the entrance to the facility and already the line was being divided by alphabetical categories. We were in the L-R category and we were third in line once we made our way there. We were greeted by an adult, who I presumed was a cadre. With the same militaristic mode of communication, Leann and I were greeted with "Good morning Sir and Ma'am, welcome this morning. Who are you here to pick up this morning?"

Leann answered, "We are here for Tony Mazziotti."

He reached for a two-way radio and blurted out to someone on the other end, "Cadet Mazziotti."

Quickly a very fuzzy reply of, "Yes, sir."

He then told us to have a seat and directed us to where Tony would be entering the room and once signed out, he could leave with us immediately. The cadre reminded us of the return check-in time.

We took our seats and watched as several cadets walked onto the large drill floor area. As I took a seat, I remembered looking into this room some months before on my first visit to the ChalleNGe and when my attention had been directed to the young cadet mopping up the floor as part of my introduction to the Youth ChalleNGe. It was the day I made the drive-in with despair, not knowing what to do next with Tony. I thought to myself how the story eventually played out from

Tony's First Visit Home

that day to this day and like a movie, I saw those moments vividly in my mind.

We sat as patiently as we could, mothers and fathers, some with a cadets' brothers and sisters, were arriving and going through the same procedure we had, just minutes before. Like us, the cadre would reach for his two-way radio and authoritatively bark out the name of the next cadet whose family had arrived. You could see the anticipation in the faces of the parents as they walked up to the cadre to ask for their son or daughter. As each family walked in, I tried to imagine what situations might have brought their son or daughter to the ChalleNGe. I wondered, too, if the fathers had felt the same pain and the same feeling of failure that I had experienced the day I brought Tony to the ChalleNGe. I examined their faces and tried to imagine what they may be thinking as they walked in to the building, here to pick up their child.

As the cadets' names were called it would take just a few minutes before they would enter the room from a large open hallway at the very back right side of the room. As a cadet appears, I look back towards the area where parents were gathered and then back at the cadet making their way towards them. Some were standing and others were seated, but when their child came into view it was special. The nervousness cemented on the parent's faces would often be replaced with enormous smiles and with eyes quickly filled with tears. The waiting family would assume the position where the last family had greeted their son or daughter as their cadet made their way through the maze of more than a hundred clear plastic bags filled with each cadets' clothes and personal items traveling with them home for the 4-day stay. Each cadet, prior to our arrival, had each placed an identification sticker on their personal bags which they lined up near the rear of the room in a long single-file line from left to right.

As the cadets came ever closer to their parents you could sense that like us they were finding it difficult to wait until all clearance was given for the cadet to join his or her family. Then, almost each cadet was greeted with hugs and kisses, with tears and with smiles, and with a welcome you might see as a soldier sees his or her family after a tour of duty in Afghanistan or Iraq. There were those young cadets who finally, after what might have seemed like months, rather than just 43 days, would almost fall into the arms of their waiting loved ones once they were granted final permission and instruction from their cadre to join their family. I could have watched all morning; but as I watched other parents greet their sons and daughters, I realized that several of those parents who had checked in after us were coming and going with their cadet.

"Leann, what do you think the holdup is?" I asked.

"I don't know, Jim. Just be patient," she replied back.

I've never been a very patient man. Another ten minutes or so had passed until I asked Leann, "should I check in again to make sure he is coming?" She knew that I what I really meant was, would you please ask if he is coming?

Leann waited until the cadre who we had checked in with had a moment free and she asked, "Sir, I know you called for our son, Tony Mazziotti, but it appears there has been some sort of delay?"

The cadre looked a bit puzzled having remembered calling Cadet Mazziotti's name perhaps 30 minutes earlier. He grabbed his radio, adjusting a button which brought out a burst of white noise and moving it towards his mouth asked whomever was on the other end, "Is Tony Mazziotti coming?"

The person on the other end replied, "Yes sir, at once sir."

He then looked at Leann and said, "Perhaps he wasn't summoned with the first request, ma'am. He should be along shortly."

We waited, perhaps, no more than three minutes until Tony emerged from the doorway as dozens of cadets had done while we had waited. Finally, it was our son. It was Tony. He was wearing a smile that extended from ear to ear. As he walked down the walkway, moving quickly towards what apparently was his bag of personal belongings, he glanced towards us with his huge smile that has always been one-of-a-kind, grabbed his bag, and continued towards us. He was wearing the standard issue green fatigue pants and a tightly fitting green tee. Tony's hair had been clipped so short that any hair was barely perceptible, and his receding hairline, clearly a "Rogge" characteristic from his mother's side of the family, stood out.

There was no question that he was excited to see us and excited to come home for the long weekend. *Thank God.* Honestly, I wasn't sure how he might appear, but this is how I had hoped it would be. His eyes glistened with apparent tears. I remember reading somewhere that there were three types of tears. There are tears of sadness, tears of hope, and tears of happiness. I believe I saw both tears of hope and tears of happiness as he came closer to us. Before he would be dismissed, it was necessary to be checked out by his platoon cadre, Mr. Demarr, who positioned himself right next to us as Tony approached.

"Good morning, Mr. and Mrs. Mazziotti. I am Mr. Demarr, your son's Cadre and squadron leader. You have quite a young man here," he said looking towards Tony. "Cadet Mazziotti," Mr. Demarr said, more a question than a statement.

Now, just a few feet from us, Tony replied, "Yes, Sir."

"Cadet Mazziotti. You know how you are to handle yourself on this visit, correct?" he asked Tony.

Yes, sir," Tony said, holding back tears and with a smile.

"Enjoy your time away and come back to us in one piece and in the right frame of mind," Mr. Demarr instructed.

"I will, sir. Thank you, sir," Tony said, all the time standing at attention and speaking with the utmost respect.

"Okay, report back on Tuesday at 1400 hours. Are we clear, cadet Mazziotti?"

"Yes sir," Tony replied.

Mr. Demarr looked at me and with a wink said to Leann and me, "Enjoy your son, I think you will see he is becoming a man."

At that moment Tony and Leann embraced. Both had tears flowing down their cheek and I wasn't far behind. I grabbed Tony and hugged him with everything I had.

"Are you ready to go home?" I asked.

"I am so ready, dad. Thank you for coming to get me!" he replied.

It was the homecoming I had hoped for. It was perfect. God, I was so happy to see Tony. We have all missed him so much

Our bags were already packed and loaded in the trunk of our car. All were ready to make Tony's Labor Day weekend something special. In my letters to him I had hinted around about our family doing a number of things for this weekend; but I wanted to exceed his expectations and keep my word. When we arrived home from the ChalleNGe, there was a warm homecoming for Tony from Nicole and Christiano. More tears. More smiles. And of course, more smiles. What a wonderful day.

"Tony," I said, "here is a list to pack. Go upstairs and grab these things and we are outta here until Saturday night."

In an earlier letter to me he had mentioned that he was hoping we wouldn't mind if he could spend some of his time home with a letter-writing girlfriend and some of his buddies. So, we arranged to spend all of Friday and Saturday with him and leave Sunday and Monday for him to hang with his friends.

"So, where are we going," he asked.

Leann, Nici, and Christiano swore to keep our plans a secret, so Leann said, "You will just have to wait and see, Tony."

We proceeded out the door, packed the trunk full of everything we needed for the next two days and headed out.

* * *

Tony's First Visit Home

Our first stop before leaving town was at a local restaurant that is notorious for great food and a lovely outdoor venue. The temperature was perfect and the skies were blue. The wind was blowing napkins around from time to time, but it was a beautiful day. Although Tony had no complaints of the food he was eating at the ChalleNGe, we wanted to make sure that he would eat great for the next few days. We were given a table outside and for more than an hour we spent time together that had been lost for the past 6 weeks or so. It was enjoyable for all of us as we listened to the stories Tony told us about the ChalleNGe. I sensed that, while still homesick and wishing he were home, he had found his place and he was experiencing success. It felt good to see him extol confidence and pride.

My kids always joked about my car. From the time I purchased it brand new out of the lot of Iowa Motor Company, I swear that my 2000 Mercury was fitted with the wrong suspension system. My kids said it was a "low rider," a term used in their circles to describe a car purposefully customized to ride just inches above the ground. You know, something that you might see in movies like American Graffiti or Grease, that centered around the late 50's and early 60's. I didn't usually take kindly to them laughing about my car, but in this case, with the five of us all loaded in the car and with the additional weight of our suitcases, I laughed along with them as we made our way over the Cascade mountains towards Salem; and every now and then hearing and feeling the car bottom out on the pavement and my brand new Continental tires rubbing against the wheel wells. Man, I'm surprised the tires didn't blow out. Normally I would have been concerned, angry actually, but not today. Today just about anything would be fine.

We arrived in Salem and made our way to McKay High School. Tony knew exactly what was going on by now. We arrived at the Royal Scots football field at about 6:30 p.m. for the scheduled 7:00 p.m. kickoff of the Mountain View High School vs. McKay to watch some of Tony's buddies, Michael

Warsaw, Hayden Maze, and his best friend, Cody Chase play. It would be his only opportunity and the last time he would be able to watch his senior class buddies play, so it was bittersweet; but he was excited!

I worried that he may feel a bit uncomfortable walking over to the stands where his friends and their families were sitting, but he showed not one bit of hesitation. Surely, Tony might be the last person anyone was expecting to see walk into that stadium, but in Tony-fashion he made his way towards the bleachers greeting and hugging friends along the way. He stopped by the sidelines to watch his former team warming up for the game, but he knew enough not to interrupt their pre-game drills. It was good to see him smiling and laughing for this one night with his friends and being able to watch the kids whom he had grown up with play ball.

All eyes of those who knew Tony were fixated on him and we were too. When he finally made his way up to where we were seated he said, "thanks, dad, I never expected this." After the game ended he walked onto the field to embrace a few of his buddies with hugs, so visibly powerful that most people might feel their ribs crack or back split in half. He even approached a couple of his former coaches, extending a hand and a smile, like a politician working a room. The only thing that appeared missing was a baby to snatch up and kiss on the forehead. To this day, I don't remember who won the game and it didn't matter. We were all just so happy to be with each other in our own little world, in the upper visitor side bleachers of the Royal Scots field. Walking out, Tony continued to say hello to a few friends that he had missed earlier. After the game, we went to get something to eat and then check in to our hotel.

We were up and at em' early on Saturday morning and as far as Tony knew we were headed home. Instead, we made our way south, past our normal exit and on towards Eugene. He knew.

Tony's First Visit Home

"Where are we headed?" He asked with a quizzical look. "Home," I said.

He looked at Christiano and then at Nici. They acted like they had no idea what he might be thinking. The more we drove, the more we began passing cars, and the more cars passing us all decked-out with the green and yellow University of Oregon Duck logo. Football fans are a little strange; at least Oregon Ducks fans are. Flags, bumper stickers, window paint, you name it.

"Are you serious," Tony asked with excitement!

For our family, the Oregon Duck games were mostly elusive. If you can get decent tickets, you know you are going to pay top dollar for a good seat and it wasn't uncommon for a good ticket to cost in excess of $100 or more. Thankfully, this was the first game of the year and against a non-threatening and non-conference opponent, so I was able to land 5 tickets for about $35 each, something I thought we could barely afford and in a seating area where we could enjoy the game. Business wasn't going well enough to spend the $700 I had estimated this weekend would cost, but I would just have to work harder, I thought, and there was absolutely no way I was not going to make this weekend special for Tony.

We arrived three hours before kickoff and we watched the parking lots fill up with tailgaters and the stadium grounds fill with tens of thousands of mostly die-hard Oregon Duck fans. There was plenty of food vendors and numerous stands selling items with the "O" or green and yellow. The game was sold out with more than 56,000 people in the stadium. Thankfully, the sky was blue and the temperature was in the 70's. The time allowed for Tony to mostly hang with Nici and Christiano, something that had been missing for a while. Leann and I kept a distance to allow them time together.

What a time we all had. Oregon won the game 48-27, but the score appeared much closer than the game really was. Tony and Christiano had a great time, as we all did, and after the game we were allowed down on the field to meet a few players and get some autographs. Tony stuck close to Christiano to make sure he located the most popular players.

After the game and on our way home, Tony must have thanked us a million times. He knew that he had seen his classmates play high school football for the very last time and he wouldn't have the opportunity to watch or listen to another Oregon Ducks game this season, since television isn't allowed at the ChalleNGe. Everything went exactly as planned.

On Sunday and Monday Tony spent most of his time with his friends. We did have a little BBQ for his friends on Sunday and everything went by so fast. It was a fantastic, heart-warming visit that allowed Leann and me to see how he had changed in just six weeks.

The break allowed for us to be with Tony until the time required to have him back by 2:00 p.m. on Tuesday. In much the same orderly fashion as performed when picking him up just a few days earlier, we dropped him back to continue on with the ChalleNGe. Upon his return, we said our goodbyes with tears and hugs and we watched him walk back to the same area from which he had appeared on Friday. He would be required to have his clear plastic bag holding his clothes and personal items searched for contraband and to have a drug test to make sure he had met the requirements of not indulging in drugs while he was home. We were asked to wait until we were given the go-ahead to leave by the cadre; if any evidence of the use of drugs was discovered in the test, Tony would be sent home immediately.

As we were sitting and waiting, we witnessed one cadet sitting with his mother engaging in a very heated discussion with one of the cadre. The door to their private meeting room was cracked enough for us to see the discussion taking place. I felt as though I was watching something I shouldn't, but I was fixated on the small room where the discussion was on-going and the emotions had taken over. The young cadet sat with his clear plastic bag with all of his belongings, his mother pleading with the cadre, her arms animatedly moving about. She was crying. Her son had his head almost in his lap. He, too, was clearly crying and shaking his head from side to side. Just a few minutes later we were given the sign that Tony had passed and that we were free to leave.

As we drove home and for days after leaving the ChalleNGe, I couldn't stop thinking about the mother we had seen crying and pleading for her son to have another chance to stay and complete the ChalleNGe Program. But I know she knew, as did we, the rules are explicit. No exceptions would be made for any cadet who failed to live up to the requirements. Nevertheless, to this day I can see her and feel the pain she must have experienced. I imagine that she knew that this might be the last chance her son would be given to finish high school. Tony told us in a letter a few days after we left that a boy had been sent home. I knew it was the boy we saw.

I hated to leave Tony there, but we all knew we had no choice. He had to complete the ChalleNGe. He now had to perform in the classroom. It would be 41 days before his next visit home and I knew that he had so much more to do.

16
LAW OF THE LID

Don't ask what the world needs. Ask what makes you come alive, and go do it. Because what the world needs is people who come alive.

Howard Thurman
African-American author & civil rights leader

I expected it. I really did. Tony had been at the ChalleNGe for some 70 days. Now, that may seem like a short time for a young man or woman to come to terms with what they want to do with their life, but keep in mind that most of the more than 150 kids that are part of each class have likely never given serious consideration to or been presented with options of what they might do once they become adults. Until now. The ChalleNGe reveals to each cadet the numerous possibilities and opportunities for them once they complete the program and graduate. Many of the cadets have heard, far too often, the things they would NEVER be able to achieve, rather than that which they can.

While most of the letters I received from Tony would bring happiness and joy to my life, there were some of the letters that left me heartsick and dispirited. One such letter came from the words of an assignment given to him by his career teacher at the ChalleNGe. The instructor had asked Tony to identify careers that he might like to explore. The careers instructor then worked with each cadet to answer their questions and help each cadet consider if they have the ability and skills or if they will be able and willing to prepare for the career of their interest. Tony had focused on several possible alternatives. He wrote down on several sheets of paper four jobs he might have an interest in. He listed an air traffic controller, construction equipment operator, and a position serving in the military.

Before entering the Oregon Youth ChalleNGe, Tony and I had occasionally talked about his interest in operating large machinery as an occupation. He seemed most interested in working in the construction industry. You know, jobs like operating backhoes, track hoes, haul trucks, end loaders, dozers, graders, rollers, and/or excavators with work in earthwork, utilities, foundation, demolition, road, or any construction work. To this, I have not one bit of experience with which to assist him in considering a path to this type of work.

I understood, I guess, what an air traffic controller does. I knew that air traffic controllers are generally individuals who are well organized, quick with numeric computations and mathematics, have assertive and firm decision-making skills, are able to maintain a cool head and composure under pressure. I'm not sure Tony fit any of those descriptive requirements, to be honest.

Then there had been his interest in serving in the military. Again, our family is not what I would classify "a military family." My father was a veteran of WWII, was a District Commander with the American Legion, and had served on the "draft board" during the Vietnam War; a truly thankless job. At the time, I might have considered serving in the military, I took notice of the draft, the burning of draft cards, and the protests on nearly every college campus in America. The country had grown tired of a cruel and punishing war and the thought of exploring opportunities in the military were replaced with the fear of being forced to serve in the military. By the time the war had come to halt, I had already made career decisions outside of military service and the country was entering a healing process with the military and war that I am not sure has healed, even today.

Tony saw the military as a place to settle in, mature, experience discipline and habit, learn job skills and serve his country. Admirable for any man or woman.

The letter was written on October 2nd and arrived at our mailbox on Thursday, October 4th. Not every letter I received from Tony was read near the ol' mailbox and sitting in my car. This one was. I will never forget it.

Tony began the letter with his usual catching-up of things going on at the ChalleNGe. The way most of his letters were. He talked about how he had missed a big outing known as a rewards trip that took all the kids to the famous and beautiful Tumalo Falls; he remained on campus because of an ankle injury and was unable to walk. He talked about how excited he was that I and a friend were coming to OYCP on the following Tuesday for the career fair.

Dad, today was a huge day. I have been doing a lot of research and a lot of talking to Cadre Demarr. Dad, I signed papers for the Marine Corps and will swear in at the United States Military Entrance Command Center in Portland shortly after graduating from OYCP. Both me and Zuniga. I have talked to the recruiter a lot with all kinds of questions. He has told me everything. He says my MOS makes bank and with the proper ASVAB score that I will be guaranteed the job! I believe you can be there when I sign my final papers and swear in... and I hope you will be, Dad. This is an opportunity of a lifetime that I took. Feel free to contact the Marine recruiter and ask him anything. His name is Sgt. Tryon and he is the local recruiter.

Man, I hope you are not upset. I just feel I am an adult and it is time for me to step up and take something that I will use for the rest of my life.

I know you are worried about me dying. Dad, that is the risk I am willing to take. I want to be the best…and let's face it.… they are the best and this is what I want to do. I love you dad.

Tony

As I sat there all I could think of was the war in Afghanistan, knowing full well that he would be taken there to fight. Not many Marines stay home when they enlist. I had seen the images on the nightly news: the caskets coming off the planes, the tears of mothers and fathers, husbands and wives, and the kids of fallen heroes. The memory of the falling towers on 9/11. I could see myself saying goodbye to him as he boarded a plane to be taken away and perhaps never return. I understand. I get it. Nearly 7000 have seen their children jet off to Iraq and Afghanistan to never return and many more will be taken as that part of the world continues to crumble in their hatred and evilness. But Tony?

He is just getting turned around. He is just now finding himself and experiencing success. When I was his age and our country was fighting the war in Vietnam, I, like every American, saw more than 58,000 young men come home in caskets or not return at all. Many more came home, never to realize their dreams, fight personal demons, deal with war injuries, and to be spat upon. God, it was a terrible thing. I didn't want the same for Tony. No parent does; but seriously, this was no time to feel sorry for myself or for Tony, for that matter. You see, I believe the choice to serve our country was the right choice for Tony. I had only hoped it might be with a branch where he was less likely to come home with severe traumatic injury or worse, dead.

Then I read more of why he made the choice. It was telling. He titled this part of his letter, "why?" It read:

Why you may ask? Why did I select the United States Marines Corps over any other branch? One of the main reasons I selected the Marine Corps is because I want to be the best. I have the utmost respect for any person that is serving or has served in the armed forces, but frankly anyone who looks at a Marine says, "Damn, the way they carry themselves, the standards they set and the discipline they have is on display. You can look over a crowd and pick a Marine out. That is how I want to be known.

All my life people have known me as lazy, a failure, and someone who doesn't give a rip about the future. When I came to the Oregon Youth ChalleNGe I learned that my future is the most important thing in my life. So, based on that, I want my future to offer an open pathway. I want to take a road that will set me up for the rest of my life. The Marine Corps is that road for me.

I looked closely at the other branches in my study. The Navy is great but does not offer a job description that excites me. The Army National Guard just doesn't fit me.

I understand that my parents will be very scared they are going to lose their first son to Operation Iraqi Freedom or in other action around the world. It is their biggest fear. As a Marine, there is that chance. I know that when I serve as a Marine people will look at me and say, "Tony is a Marine. Tony is a disciplined individual. Tony knows how to carry himself and Tony is not a failure."

I need all the support I can get!

Along with this, he attached a Pros and Cons sheet. A detailed list. As I looked at it, I realized that he had spent considerable time and effort thinking through this decision. I know Cadre Demarr, Tony's OYCP Platoon Leader and a former Marine himself, wasn't necessarily excited for Tony's consideration and choice. As a Marine, he experienced it first-hand. I knew he had worked diligently to help Tony make the right choice for Tony.

The sheet listed 18 reasons to be a Marine. It listed nine reasons not to join. Smart reasons. Rationale reasons. Reasons that were important to him.

I realized as I read the list that Tony had spent more time in outlining his career path than anyone I had ever known, including me. Never had I ever carefully and systematically taken as much care as he had. I thought about my selection in a college to attend. My selection to attend Upper Iowa University was based on receiving a full ride music scholarship, but never did I look at all the pros and cons of my decision. My choice to work in the family business was never about pros and cons. My decision to do so was based on the easy choice and perhaps even the choice everyone else wanted me to make.

As a teacher and coach of real estate agents every single day, I know that few take the time to list the "Why" they decided to become a real estate agent and certainly even fewer have a business plan looking at the pros and cons of working with specific types of properties, buyers, and sellers. Seldom might you see the words "strategic thinking" and "Realtors" in the same sentence. The fact is, more than 50% of all real estate agents fail to renew their license after just their first two years in the business and 87% leave the business after their fifth year and after working to secure the required clock hours and education credits to pass the real estate examination in their state and become a Realtor. Now, that isn't well thought out, wouldn't you agree?

I do know that Tony had done his homework. I know that the OYCP helped him through careful career planning to do exactly that. Nevertheless, reading his letter on this cool Thursday afternoon in October wasn't easy. More than a million young men and women serve in our military around the world. Thousands enlist each year. I am certainly not the first dad to have his son inform him that his future plans included a date certain to sign documents and to give his solemn oath to service his country. But, this was my Tony. The Tony who, perhaps, had finally discovered himself.

One of my favorite books, *Winners Never Cheat*, by Jon Huntsman, an incredible human being, by the way, spoke of one thought that comes to my mind. Huntsman said, "some people earn admiration and respect. If you must choose one, however, go for respect every time." There was little doubt that Tony felt he hadn't captured either until putting it all on the line and walking into the Oregon Youth ChalleNGe ready to write a new history for himself. Surely, he would earn the admiration of many by completing the Youth ChalleNGe and by becoming a United States Marine.

I have read and written down many quotes and words of others that seem to speak to me. One passage written in my journal notes came from a website for parents of Marines. It read, "Most of us can only stand on the sidelines and watch the transformation from recruit to Marine. Unless you have become a Marine through the grit and tough training of boot camp, you cannot possibly fully comprehend Esprit de Corps and the Core Values. However, you will come to understand that these new philosophies are not easily achieved, and therefore, command the greatest respect from those of us on the sidelines."

Tony would earn my respect and as Jon Huntsman pointed out, there may be nothing as important as earning the respect of others.

17
HELPING TO SHAPE MY SON'S LIFE

My task, which I am trying to achieve is, by the power of the written word, to make you hear, to make you feel--it is, before all, to make you see.

Joseph Conrad

It was Day 101, October 27th. It sure seemed like much longer than that. Today was Saturday. Leann was at work, Christiano and Nici were still in bed. After all, Saturdays are perfect days to sleep-in, right? For whatever reason, when I looked at my table clock in the bedroom it read 6:44 a.m. I was wide awake so I tracked downstairs.

As I made my way down the stairway the neighborhood opened up through the front living room, front dining room, and front door windows. I made my way to the front door to scope out the morning that greeted me and I could see it was sunny and cold without even sticking my finger out the door. The skimpy trees in front of our house were blowing from side to side and two doors down, the rental house had sprinklers in high intensity mode blowing water that must have been no more than one degree warmer than the freezing point, over an already icy lawn. I thought how today, especially this morning, might be a perfect time to sit down and write to Tony. Too cold to take the dog anywhere. Too cold to go for a walk. Best of all, it was quiet.

I guess I didn't have a set routine in approaching my writing to Tony each day. I just wrote. As I have said, I wanted to be sure to keep my letters as uplifting as day-to-day life from home can be. You understand. Day-to-day life can be monotonous and really uneventful. Man, ours is at least. I was careful about what news regarding family, friends, and even personal challenges I would speak of in my letters. However, I did want to make sure he walked with me on my personal business stubble. I wrote of it, not to burden him with my problem or problems, but to let him know he wasn't alone in dealing with life issues. I hoped he might look in the mirror each day and maybe even see me standing behind him; sometimes struggling, tired, lonely and facing problems just like he was.

Many times, before putting pen to paper, I would just sit and absorb what he would be saying to Leann and me in his letters. I would often re-read the letters I had written to him, knowing hindsight is 20/20. I found writing, most days using my computer, would allow me to save and easily read them again later. Sometimes I would read what I had written and ask myself why I said things the way I did. It is kind of like talking into a voice recorder and taping yourself. When you are finished and play back the tape, if you are like most people, you will say, "That doesn't sound anything like me. Do I really sound like that?" Actually, there is a whole science thing to how you hear your voice and how others hear you. Anyway, that is how I look at these letters, but without the acoustical science thing, of course.

And yes, sometimes I would think, "Did I really say that?" If a prior letter from the day or week before didn't hit the mark or failed to offer the love and support I intended to express, I would try to write it better later. Let's face it. Before writing to Tony each day I hadn't written a letter since I went to college in the 70's, perhaps to my girlfriend, and even that was rare. I have never been apart for much more than a few days from Leann in our 37-plus years of marriage, so letter writing wasn't exactly my forté. I was new to this whole letter writing and expression in words deal.

As I picked up my pen, I reflected on how Tony's letters seemed to be mostly filled with optimism and confidence over the past weeks. He was finding success in the classroom. He had been given leadership roles among his peers and he could see the light at the end of the tunnel. I wondered, however, if he was happy. We all know we can experience success without truly being happy. Millions of adults do it every day by getting in their cars and heading to work. If success is measured by income perhaps they are successful, but how many are really happy? There is little doubt that we live in a country where the accumulation of personal wealth is far more important than our own personal happiness and the happiness of others, wouldn't you agree?

Next to my chair was "my bag." My bag holds several books and dozens of notes, articles cut from newspapers, and hand-written papers that were mostly dog-eared and wrinkled, but holding valuable words; at least valuable to me. I had learned some time before from an audio tape I had listened to featuring John C. Maxwell, that his secret to writing was always jotting down thoughts of his own and the words and thoughts of others. He would often place them carefully in a small file tucked into a drawer at his desk and categorized by topic or relevance so they might be available at a moment's notice. While I wasn't quite that organized and still am not, I have what my wife calls, "piles" everywhere around the house. I have favorite magazines that hold gems of information. I have collections of articles torn from newspapers and magazines in another pile. I have cassette tapes, DVD's, CD's, you name it. All have their special place. Leann doesn't much care for my filing system.

Today I went to "my bag" looking for something I had copied from somewhere a long time ago. *There it is.* I had failed to note on the paper the author and for the life of me I couldn't, and still can't, give credit where credit is surely due. It had been awhile, but before finding it in my bag I remembered its content and relevance for this day. I even think I had jotted down my own perspectives.

I want to make sure Tony considers the importance of happiness in his life and I am wondering if maybe happiness is not a key focus point at the ChalleNGe? I know the focus of the ChalleNGe was towards academic excellence, responsible citizenship, physical fitness, leadership, job skills, service, health, hygiene, and life coping skills. I get it. I can't disagree with the program's initiatives and goals; but, today I wanted Tony to hear about Happiness. I am hoping you, too, will benefit from the writing.

Tony,

If you're looking to improve your life, it generally means that you're not satisfied with your current life. Nothing wrong with that, Tony. Seeking to improve your life means understanding you can have more, do more and be more. It means realizing the massive potential within you. It means having the courage to follow your dreams. Much like your mother and I did when we picked up from a perfectly okay life to move to Oregon. We followed our dreams. You must too.

As a dreamer with big dreams, I've spent a lot of my time thinking about how I want my future to be. Probably too much time, Tony. I've fallen into the trap of thinking I'll be happy when I achieve this or that and have been left frustrated at my lack of progress from time to time. If you dream of a better life but are unhappy with now, you'll never achieve your dreams.

You see, this second, this minute is the only time that really exists. Your past has happened and your future depends largely on what you think now. Right now. Think unhappy thoughts and you're sending out negative emotions that can stop you progressing. Being unhappy can grow your fears and increase your stress. So just as you have to choose your thoughts carefully, you can also choose your emotions. In fact, it's the emotions behind the thoughts that will ultimately take you towards your dreams, or away from it. Choose happiness.

It also goes beyond that. Want more in your life… but be grateful for what you have. The only way you want is to appreciate what you have now… Here's something you can try……

Just before you go to sleep tonight think about all the things you are grateful for in your life. Also, be grateful for all the things you want in your life as if you already have them. For example, be grateful for the roof over your head, your family, friends, the ChalleNGe…and include the best-selling book you are going to write, or the shiny new car on your list as though they already exist in your current reality. This can be extremely powerful and kick start your subconscious into making dreams real. Try it.

One more thing. Too much dreaming can kill your dreams.

Dreaming, visualizing your future can help your dreams come real. In fact, all the big achievers in life have been dreamers. But too much time spent daydreaming about the future and you're not living in the present. Be 100 percent in the present and it will help you focus 100% on your goals and achieve much more. It will help you be more organized, more attentive and more efficient.

So if you are struggling to make progress on your dreams, remember these key points:

- *Controlling your future, means controlling your present.*
- *Plan your time for dreaming and your time for being 100 percent in the present.*
- *And...be happy now as this is the only way you can be happy in the future.*

I love you, Tony.

Dad

A day before Halloween, Tony sent a letter mentioning Thanksgiving.

October 30th

Tomorrow is Halloween. I think we have a big dinner and that's all. We ran a good 6 miles today. I'm frickin' burnt out. I am sending my Central Oregon Community College application home, so look it over and get it in if you would. Twenty-one days until break. I can't wait. Please call Cody. I would like for him to come with you to pick me up. This break should be pretty relaxed. Lots of good food, church, maybe a night out with the boys and watching as much football as possible. I miss you all and can't wait to spend time with you and getting ready for graduation and starting school up again.

Tony

Then his letter on Halloween October 31st:

Hey Pop,

Shit! today has sucked so frickin' bad. The platoon was horrible this morning and...well...we are back on Pre-ChalleNGe like treatment. It is worse than before, but it is cool with me and Zuniga. We just tell each other it's extra PT and big dumb asses in black shirts who yell a lot! Basically it means we are back in all sweats while the rest of the company is in their camis. Everything is back to "by the numbers." It's easy for me, I've got their game down. So, oh well. Just 19 days till I come home and I can't wait. Now that I'm almost done with school I can't wait to get out of here! Maybe it's not me speaking because I am so pissed off at my platoon and it is times like today that I wish I had never come to the ChalleNGe.

I miss you dad. I love you. Be home soon.

Tony

His letters sent the day before Halloween and another on Halloween were only the second time I could remember that he had expressed real displeasure with the ChalleNGe outside of the first two-week pre-ChalleNGe period. Listen, it's not going to be paradise whenever you put a lot of kids in a small area, away from home, and for any length of time at all. The fact is, when one cadet messes up, they all pay the price. Plus, we all have bad days, right?

The point is that the Youth ChalleNGe isn't a perfect place. No place is. I had to keep that in mind. I knew that even the bad days were necessary for this experience because life was going to hit him square across the side of the head once he left the ChalleNGe. Sure, he was, like we are, going to have some bad experiences at the ChalleNGe. I had to hope he wouldn't allow the bad experiences to fester and become worse.

I am reminded of a time when on Saturday afternoons there was likely only one channel on television where you could watch a sporting event. If you remember ABC's Wide World of Sports, you know what I am talking about. No cable with dozens of sporting events. Usually just one. The show was hosted by Jim McKay and was on from 1961 thru 1998. The show would open with his voice saying, "Spanning the globe to bring you the constant variety in sports…the thrill of victory and the agony of defeat." With his words "agony of defeat" and a musical arpeggio indicating a downward fall, the viewers would see the horrific video tape of a ski jumper heading down a ski ramp and suddenly go head over heels in a horrendous and brutal crash. His body looked like a limp noodle as it crashed through a support structure and then bouncing off the ground.

For years, I watched that show intro over and over again. Each time was as bad as the time before. Surely, this was at the very least a career ending skiing accident. What most people didn't know was that skier Vinko Bogataj's frightening fall wasn't an accident at all. Earlier in the day he had actually landed an incredible jump of 410 feet at the 1970 World Ski Flying Championships. A fabulous jump it was. As the day progressed, the ski jump had become icy, very icy, in fact. As he was going down the ramp, he was picking up so much speed that if he had completed the jump he might have landed far beyond the prepared landing area and died.

So, instead of following through with a landing that might have killed him, he decided to practically sit and abort the jump, flying off the end of the ramp itself. His last-minute decision, which appeared to be catastrophic, actually saved his life. The crash resulted in what he said was a severe headache and some sore muscles!

Life is like that and I hoped Tony, like Vinko, wouldn't allow his bad experience or experiences to become something even worse. Life can do that to people. Vinko Bogataj could have quit and put the skis away and allowed his experience to haunt him for life. He didn't. He competed many more times, and while never a world champion himself, Bogataj became a ski instructor, coaching the 1991 World Champion Slovenian ski jumper Franci Petek.

I needed to help Tony focus not on what wasn't working, but on where he wanted to go and what he wanted to achieve. My letter on Day 113 read:

Tony,

Here is the deal. You are going to build a house. So, where do you start? Well, you have to purchase land to build it on, right? You have to know that you can get water from the city or place a well on the property. How about sewage? How are you going to get to and from your house? Are there roads? How about schools for your kids or shopping for your family? Is there a hospital nearby? How big of a house will you build? How many rooms? How many bathrooms? Do you need permits to build it? How big will the kitchen be? And the cabinets in the kitchen? A two-car garage? A driveway? Will you plant trees and landscape the lot? Who will you hire to build it? How much will it cost? Where will you purchase the materials?

Tony, you can see how much planning goes into building a house, right? Now ask yourself how many people spend as much time planning their life as they do planning their house? The answer is, Few. That is why you really need to plan out your life, Tony.

What will your plan be? It is up to you, Tony. Now is the time to build your masterpiece. The YOU masterpiece.

I see it all the time in my business, almost every day. Real estate agents who will work side-by-side with a client diligently assisting them in planning how they will purchase the land and build the home, assisting even in helping them select the colors and the finishes down to the last detail. However, in their own lives they haven't spent any time at all building their "business masterpiece." Why is that?

Why do most of us spend more time planning our summer vacations than we do with our own lives? I knew I didn't want this for Tony and for this five months I had the opportunity to help shape his life, I thought.

18
A PERFECT DAY

If you're not in the parade, you watch the parade. That's Life.

Mike Ditka

It was frigid, almost bone-chilling cold on the morning of Saturday, November 10th. On our calendar, it was Day 115 of Tony's journey. Veterans Day would be celebrated on this day in Bend. Our family often ventured downtown for the annual parade through Main Street in Bend. The Veterans Day parade is still a big deal in our small town. It is easily one of the largest parades in all of Oregon, some say west of the Mississippi, and on this day the city would be dedicating the new Veterans Memorial Bridge, the Randy Newman Memorial Walkway, and giving special recognition to Gulf War veterans. Thousands will gather along the lovely streets embellished with hundreds of flags along the parade route. In fact, for this parade, more than 170 flags that were flown over the U.S. Capitol would be part of those waving.

We knew, from having attended prior Parades, that the Oregon Youth ChalleNGe would be everywhere downtown.... and they were. The OYCP kids were clad in their fatigues along with their standard issue caps and gloves. You couldn't miss them. They were posted at every intersection along the parade route to assist the police department with traffic and pedestrian concerns. They were along the bridges on the route making sure to watch for a youngster that might dart out in front of a parade float, car, tractor, and even horses. This is the northwest and a parade without plenty of horses, rodeo queens from the summer past, and cowboy hats isn't a parade.

It was a Saturday and neither Leann nor I had to work. My plan was to arrive downtown and scour the streets for any evidence of cadets from the ChalleNGe with the hope of catching a glimpse of Tony. Just being able to see him would be enough, but I had spoken to his superiors earlier about the prospect of our likely coming in contact with Tony at a Bend function. The OYCP is very active in our community and in attendance at many events where manpower and volunteerism is vital. We would, from time to time, see OYCP buses and vehicles traveling past us headed to help with one of dozens of Central Oregon events. His superiors asked that should I be in attendance at a function where Tony was present to approach them and alert them to our being there.

"If it is appropriate and time allows, we can grant you a few minutes to say hello to your son," Cadre Demarr has told me. The cadets always came in clearly identified buses from the OYCP facility. I remembered seeing them in previous years and my reticula activator was full on. I would be able to spot anything remotely close to OYCP.

We arrived downtown a little after 8:00 a.m., three hours before the official start of the parade. I wasn't going to lose an opportunity to see Tony, and even better yet, hopefully, have the opportunity to see his face, put my arms around him, and of course, tell him how much we missed him, loved him, and were proud of him. There was still plenty of frost on the bike racks and metal street poles. I had dressed in layers, wore two pair of gloves, and was ready to wait it out. I had, however, forgotten a hat. Just plain dumb.

Once we had parked our car, I made my way up and down the parade route. There were participants scurrying to get to the start point for the Veterans Day/Marine Corps 5K Run, some in just running shorts and T-shirts. I couldn't begin to imagine how cold they were. My ears were about to fall off. Someone had clearly claimed my toes, for there was no evidence of any feeling in them. The four of us kept warm by moving and walking, looking for Tony and his ChalleNGe family of about 150 youth and their superiors.

Then, at about 9:15 a.m. we saw two OYCP buses pull up about a block or so in front of us, near the parade route start point.

"They are here!" I remember Nici yelling and pointing in the direction of the buses.

"Okay," I said. "Let's just slowly make our way in that direction. I don't want to cause any distraction for the cadre and overstep our being able to talk to Tony." It seemed like my ears weren't nearly as cold at that moment and I certainly had forgotten about my toes, which I was convinced were about to fall off just a few minutes earlier.

As they were making their way off the buses, we continued to make our way towards them, but stopping about 40 yards from where the cadre were firmly shouting out orders and instructions. Each cadet was dressed exactly the same as the others. Their caps made it difficult to see faces and the boys all have the same haircut, so our only identifier from 40 yards would be his tall 6' 4" frame. They kept unloading and we continued to hold our place just across the street. Every once and a while one of us would say, "There he is!" with excitement and big smiles, only to realize it wasn't him. Finally, he shuffled off the bus, looking straight ahead and moving exactly in the direction of the formation being described by his superiors. Yep, it was him, but we would stay back until the cadre completed their instructions.

Once it appeared that we would no longer be intruding on official OYCP business, we moved slowly toward the group. We were maybe twenty yards from the group when I made eye contact with Cadre Demarr, Tony's superior and company leader. There was a mutual head nod indicating that he knew I was standing by with my family and waiting to say hello to his cadet and my son. After a few minutes, I heard him shout out, "Mazziotti!"

Almost immediately I could see the movement from one of the lines that apparently included Tony, and then he emerged out of the group, standing at attention, front and center with Cadre Demarr. "Yes sir," my son said with confidence and respect.

"Mr. Mazziotti, you may take five minutes to step out of line and speak with your parents. Make sure you tell your mother that you love her," Cadre Demarr said.

"Yes, sir, thank you sir," Tony barked back.

At that moment Cadre Demarr looked my way once again and with a wink of his eye let us know that all was okay. As Tony reached us I let his mother, Nici, and Christiano all hug and kiss him before I greeted him. I stood back enjoying watching the smiles on everyone's face.

With each greeting one another, I couldn't help but look over the shoulder of my wife and seeing a number of cadets, left standing, awaiting further instructions from their Cadre, but seeing Tony experiencing the love of his family. I thought for a minute how hard it must have been for some of them to see one of their own having the opportunity to see his parents and family on a non-scheduled visitation. Did they feel sadness? Were they missing their family as much as Tony had missed us these first 120 days or so? Was I just seeing more spilling out of their eyes and faces and seemingly their hearts than what was really there? I felt badly for them, but I was selfishly not willing to bypass the opportunity to spend the time granted to me and my family to spend time with Tony.

Normal handshakes no longer sufficed for greetings between us. Handshakes had been replaced by hugs and not short how-do-you-do type hugs. Our hugs were genuine, heartfelt, and big. Really big! It would be all that we had to hold on to until we would be able to be together again. Finally, it was my turn. Only warmth surrounded me. He looked good. He looked happy. He looked confident and he looked like I hoped my son would look.

We spent five minutes just asking about one another, but the person perhaps needing the most that morning might not have been Tony, but instead his little brother. Christiano seldom complained about Tony being gone from home, but it was clearly an empty spot in his life. In many ways, I know he was relieved that the yelling had stopped and the disappointment and sadness had halted from when Tony was home; but so were the summer months, the baseball games without his older brother present to cheer him on or to help him, if simply by playing a game of catch with a glove and a ball or a pigskin in the street in front of our house on Oakview Drive. Missing was his older brother to see him make a sensational block or a spectacular tackle on a cool crisp day in Central Oregon. A 12-year-old boy needs his older brother.

I didn't want to take advantage and visit with Tony more than I thought might be acceptable to his cadre. Who knows, I thought. Maybe there will be other opportunities to see Tony while working in the community with his fellow cadets. So, after the five minutes we hugged, kissed, and let him walk back to join the others from OYCP. After all, it was only 10 days until his Thanksgiving break where he would be able to spend five and a half days with us.

Before he walked away I asked him, "So what duty do you have today?"

"I don't know," he said. "They haven't given us our assignments yet. I'll probably be asked to secure an intersection or something."

"Oh, okay," I replied. "So, you don't have to march in the parade or anything?"

He said, "Nope, the honor guard does that and hey, you will have to watch for Demetri! He is marching!"

Demetri had become a close friend at the ChalleNGe. The two of them were both members of the same squad and both had competed to earn the squadron leader. When it came down to the selection, Demetri won the position and there were no hard feelings. In fact, they supported each other at every opportunity they were given. We had met Demetri in late August as the cadets were being dismissed for the Labor Day weekend, so we knew what he looked like so we could easily pick him out as they would march.

"Well, okay," I said. "Maybe we will just hang back and see where you are going and watch the parade from an area near you. Is that okay?"

He replied, "Sure, I don't see a problem with it. If it is a problem I'll let you know, dad," he said.

As we said goodbye, I watched as he walked back to join the others. The group was still lined up and receiving instructions from the Cadre as they made their final plans for the parade. Tony took his place in line from where he had just left a few minutes earlier. An aura of respect was evident as we stood waiting for the cadets to disburse. It wasn't like an ordinary school where you would see kids darting in and out of position from where they had been asked to stand and wait, boys pushing and playfully punching one another, kids starring downward towards their phone in an almost hypnotic state where they were consumed with almost endless texting and tweeting, or teachers repeatedly asking or begging for their attention. Discipline was evident here. The cadre demanded respect and got it!

At about 9:45 a.m. the cadets began to go in different directions, mostly in groups of four or so. Some being accompanied by a Cadre from the ChalleNGe and others with just their group. Tony made his way with six other Cadre having crossed the street from us and walking north towards the Bank of the Cascades main branch where Leann had worked for five years.

We followed at a comfortable distance behind so as not to stalk our own son or prevent him from carrying out his duties. When he got to the bank he headed west and took a position at the bridge that was being dedicated officially immediately following the parade as the Veterans Memorial Bridge. His job was standing near the middle of the bridge to make sure no one darted out in front of the parade participants or worse, climb up on the decorative concrete railings and fall into the Deschutes River below.

We waited a few minutes and then made our way to claim our spot to view the parade right next to where Tony would be standing. We laughed at some of the floats, admired many of the cars, and of course, commented on girls in the parade. From time to time someone passing by would recognize Tony and yell out his name! He, unlike the other cadets, was a hometown boy. It was perfect. At exactly 11:00 a.m., an F15 flew over us, at what seemed to be close enough to touch, and the parade began. Veterans Day parades always start with a fly-over.

For the next two plus hours we were able to talk to Tony and enjoy added time together that we had never expected. I would stand with Tony for a while, then his mother might spend a few minutes with him. Christiano and Nici both were able to talk and joke with him as well. It was heart-warming to watch them joke and laugh together.

We talked about so many things. The last time we had been able to visit with him was on visitation day on October 7th, so we had more than a months' worth of catching up to do. He spoke about his studies, his teachers, his cadre, his new friends, and even some thoughts about his future, namely joining the ROTC. It was clear that he was comfortable and achieving like never before. Here, he wasn't simply given assignments by his teachers, rather, he was given assignments, required to complete them, and turn them in on time, every time. Much was and is expected of the cadets. Nothing except their best is acceptable or tolerated. Period.

As the parade came to an end, we left him to gather with his "bridge group" of cadets and return to the buses. As the four of us made our way back to where we had parked our car, dodging in and out of the hoard of people all seemingly going in the opposite direction than us, we all commented on how good he looked, how happy he seemed to be, and of course, how proud we all were of him.

We climbed in our car, relieved to thaw our cold extremities and enjoy the heat blowing out of the vents. Once on our way home, we decided to stop by McDonald's to grab something to eat. As I was standing at the counter waiting to place our order, I wondered if Tony had gotten on the bus to return to the ChalleNGe and then I realized that the buses would be making their way right past us on their way back. I grabbed Christiano and we ran outside to the south side of the building facing the highway that the buses would travel on. We waited and waited and finally we could see the buses coming.

We both stood there in the cold hoping to catch one final brief look at Tony. I remember seeing our breath as we were both breathing hard from our sprint to the hill overlooking the highway. The buses passed much too fast for my liking. While I didn't want to embarrass Tony, both Yanno and I waved. Yanno, a bit more enthusiastically than me, but both of us using our entire arm instead of the parade-like hand waves that we had just witnessed. You know, the hand wave where a person just moves their hand above their wrist ever so slightly, looking almost like a mannequin in the women's department store at Macy's. Our waves probably looked more like the ones you would expect from someone trying to wave down a plane from a deserted island after months of captivity!

A couple cadets waved back, but I couldn't see their faces clear enough to know if it was Tony or just another cadet or two politely waving back to a couple of people standing on the side of the road who were waving at them.

As I stood there I realized that I had been able to see Tony just about anytime I wanted for the past 18 years leading up to his leaving for the ChalleNGe. And maybe I...and maybe you...appreciate the joy of being able to look, really look at those we love often enough. Oh sure, we see them, but do we really see them and realize how lucky we are to have them in our lives. I swore that would not happen again.

Could everything be going as well as it appeared? Only time would tell. It had been a perfect day and we knew we would see Tony in just a couple of weeks for Thanksgiving break.

19
A THANKSGIVING OF MIXED FEELINGS

The pleasure of expecting enjoyment is often greater than that of obtaining it, and the completion of almost every wish is found a disappointment.

Samuel Johnson
English poet

Thanksgiving break came on Wednesday, November 21st and we were scheduled to pick up Tony from the ChalleNGe at 0800 hours! As excited as I was, as our entire family was, I was a little bit apprehensive about this visit. I can't explain it. I guess it was just a culmination of his time away, the worry....

Paul Tillich's book, *The Courage To Be*, came to mind as I prepared for Tony's upcoming visit. When asked, Tillich said his book was about real courage and saying 'yes to life' even in the face of hardship and the pain we experience. He spoke about how it takes courage to find something positive and something meaningful about ourselves and life every day. Well, it was my hope that Tony had the courage Tillich spoke of and that he was in fact saying *yes* to life, but I wasn't sure if he had or was. The next five days with him would tell us a lot, I thought.

The instructions given to us clearly stated that only parents and/or guardians were allowed to pick up the cadets for the Thanksgiving break. Nici and Christiano stayed at home as Leann and I made our way east of Bend to the ChalleNGe facility. This was our third "official" visit to the ChalleNGe listed on the OYCP calendar where we were able to come and bring him home: the first on Labor Day, the second in October, where we were able to take him off campus for six hours before returning him, and today.

It was 7:30 a.m. when we left home. As we drove the few miles I noticed that my hands were damp and clammy on the steering wheel of my car. My hands are never that way. I wasn't sure if it was nervousness or anxiousness or both. Again, we were met with a line of cars in the driveway of the OYCP. Eighteen to be exact. We learned from the last time in coming to pick up Tony for a visit that each cadet would be called to come to the check-out area once his parents or guardian checked in. Tony wouldn't have to wait long. The line moved quickly. It was cool, but not cold. Each cadet had his or her belongings lined up in clear plastic bags to bring home for the long break. He would be home for four full days, returning on Monday, November 26th.

Just like our two prior visits to pick up Tony, we stepped up to the check-in area to identify ourselves and to request that Tony be released. This time our wait wasn't long at all, maybe three minutes after his name was called. Before he arrived, his Platoon Cadre, Mr. Demarr, spotted Leann and me and walked over to us extending his hand and welcoming us with a confident smile and a firm handshake. "Marines," I thought to myself with exacerbation! Seems like every marine I have ever met has at least double the strength of my handshake.

He asked politely, "How are you folks doing?"

A Thanksgiving of Mixed Feelings

"Great, Mr. Demarr, thank you for asking," I replied. "So, how is Tony doing?"

He smiled and said, "I enjoy being around Tony, sir. He is doing well and, as you know, is hell bent on becoming a Marine when he leaves here in December."

"Yep, I know Mr. Demarr, "I said.

He replied, "Well, you may know I served in the Marine Corps and I want you to know that while I love the Marine Corps and the opportunities it provided to me, I don't know that I would suggest entering the Marine Corps as the right thing for anyone right now, especially with the wars in the Middle East."

"Yes, I know Mr. Demarr. I know this is something he feels he needs to do for himself and our country. I would much rather he look at a service branch that might be a little safer, but it is his decision." I said to him.

"Yes, sir. He has spoken to the recruiter and I think his mind is made up," he said.

At that moment, we all spotted Tony. He was wearing a huge smile and walking briskly. He looked in our direction and smiled even wider. My nervousness and anxiousness were replaced with relief and excitement. Tony walked to the area where his belongings were located and grabbed his bag and headed our way. As he approached his Platoon Leader Cadre, Mr. Demarr, took on a little different demeanor.

As Tony walked up to us Mr. Demarr looked at Tony and asked, "You ready to go home Mr. Mazziotti?"

"Yes sir," Tony answered back with respect and almost at attention.

"Mr. Mazziotti, please go home today and do the right things. Do you understand?" asked Mr. Demarr?

"Yes, sir" Tony replied.

"Great. Treat your parents with respect, behave, and come back ready to complete the ChalleNGe. Okay?" he said to Tony.

"Yes sir, I will sir," Tony reassured him.

"Alright, get out of here," Mr. Demarr concluded with a clear grin on his face and a wink of his eye towards Leann and me.

I again shook his hand while Tony hugged his mother and off we went, but not before I put my arms around Tony and hugged him so he knew I meant it. And, I did. Hopefully, this was the beginning to a great Thanksgiving weekend. As we walked to the car I noticed that Tony was carrying what seemed to me to be a lot to bring home for a four-day visit.

I said to him, "So, what the heck do you have in that bag, Tony? It looks like it must weigh 100 pounds."

"Only a few weeks to go Dad," he grunted, obviously carrying a heavy load. "They gave us a list of what we needed to finish up and told us to bring the rest home with us."

He then pulled out a list of things he wanted to do over the Thanksgiving break. It was obvious that he had given his time home a lot of thought. Among the top items were things most teenagers take for granted every day. The list included:

- Listen to music
- Watch football
- (Drink) the new monsters
- Go to Best Buy
- Make a CD
- Run and PT with Christiano
- Have Mom make enchiladas
- Go to church

Seems pretty simple doesn't it.

The minute Tony sat down in the car in the OYCP parking lot I could detect that, while he was happy to be coming home for the weekend, he seemed tired and just plain worn. I don't know, maybe he was exhausted, but he didn't express his coming home with the excitement I might have expected.

"Glad to be coming home, Tony?" I asked him.

"Dad, I am just glad that upon returning on Monday there will be 23 days remaining," he answered back.

"Been a long haul, huh Tony?"

"Yea, I am looking forward to finishing up classes and coming home. It has been hard, really hard, Dad." he said.

Finally, we pulled up in front of the house. Both Nici and Christiano darted out the front door to greet Tony and to share kisses and hugs and a warm welcome. Smiles were plentiful. At times like this I would realize just how much both Nici and Christiano had been impacted by Tony begin away for such a long time. Especially Christiano.

More than Nici, Christiano was with Leann and me most of the time when he wasn't in school. He heard our every word and concern about Tony, felt our every disappointment, and experienced our almost continuous conversations about Tony. Gosh, he was just a 12-year-old who, while never ignored, understood where our focus had been for these many weeks and long before. I tried to imagine how he felt inside when Tony climbed out of the car for the holiday weekend. I'm not sure I ever asked him how he felt about this day and about the past weeks and months. I should have.

Trust me, I am not into the "rumination" which is a focused attention on bad feelings and experiences from the past; although to write this book took some of that. I mean, I think we all have regrets and questions about the past and things we wish we would have said and maybe done; but, among other things, I will always wonder if I communicated, cared for, focused enough on Christiano during this time. In her book, *Execution is The Strategy*, Laura Stack say's that part of her strategy in life is to not fret about past mistakes. She says, "Sure, you've made mistakes in the past, but don't let that stop you from proceeding boldly." Maybe I would change her words to read "Sure, you've made mistakes in the past, but don't let that stop you from living every next day working to improve on the last."

Leann had prepared enough food to feed an army. Tony had requested a few of Leann's specialties during his break, and of course, Leann accommodated him. Of everything Leann prepares in the kitchen, Tony's favorite is home-made enchiladas and Leann had several pans ready for the oven. The refrigerator was full, the pantry was stocked with every type of Dorito and potato chip variety imaginable; there was plenty of soda and a variety of sports drink flavors that he had consumed so much of throughout the years be played ball in middle and high school.

Christiano had worked for hours preparing an extensive report, complete with pictures and newspaper articles, on the University of Oregon Ducks football team. I don't think Tony had been inside the front door for more than three seconds before Yanno grabbed it and placed it in Tony's hands. Nici was anxious to tell him about her 5th grade class at Vern Patrick Elementary and her experiences as a first-year teacher. I had, of course, prepared a minute-by-minute detailed schedule for every football game that would be on television for the next few days, knowing how much he missed watching football, let alone not been able to play it in his final year of high school.

Tony had asked if we could go to our local military surplus store, always a favorite place for him and the kids to go. He was looking for boots of some type, but with a size 14 shoe, a trip was usually unsuccessful. This would be the case on this visit. All was not lost because he also needed to purchase a white shirt and black pants for his upcoming graduation from OYCP. We were also going to attempt to purchase some dress shoes, unless a pair of mine might fit him. Thankfully, a trip to our local Wal-Mart provided everything he needed.

Late in the afternoon and after dinner Tony asked if he could spend some time with his friends. While I might have wanted to spend every minute with him I knew how much he had missed his buddies. Thankfully, he had just a week or so earlier broken off his relationship (or vice versa) with his girlfriend. I'm not sure what happened between the two of them, but I knew, and often commented in my letters to him, that he needed to really think about the relationship with her. He was aware of my opinions about her. She was a beautiful girl, but just plain bad for him. I know the last thing a young man wants is to hear the advice of his father regarding someone he may think he loves. While he was working to change his life, she continued engaging in behavior that had helped secure his path to the ChalleNGe. Hopefully, he and his buddies wouldn't do something stupid while he was home, but he was ready for the challenges he would be facing in less than a month. Off he went and returned home ready for bed around 11 p.m.

The next few days didn't go the way we had hoped and imaged it might. Tony seemed distant and not himself. He expressed little joy and what joy he did express seemed forced and distant. He spent much of his time with his friends, which of course was expected, and all but what seemed to be just a few hours at home.

Thanksgiving Day, however, was a good day. Tony helped and took part in preparing the turkey with a crazy *"Kidd Kraddicks Famous Brown Bag Turkey Recipe"* that Nici and Christiano had heard about on the Kid Kraddick Radio Show. They all got into the spirit of their contribution to the Thanksgiving meal and I must admit, it was perhaps one of the top three best turkeys I have ever eaten. Christiano pleasured in cutting up onions and carrots. Tony handled the celery chopping and garlic placement. Nici handled rubbing the turkey with olive oil and other miscellaneous requirements. They all helped and watched as the turkey was placed in a roasting pan, barely accommodating the huge turkey, covering it with a large brown paper bag and then stapling it shut, which frankly scared me to death that a staple would end up clinging to the back of my throat or something even worse.

Besides the staples, I was suspicious of the paper bag starting a fire in the oven. Certainly, it wouldn't be beyond the antics of Kidd Kraddick to set up his listening audience across the United States for a Thanksgiving they might never forget featuring a flaming fiery turkey event. He certainly was known for gags and practical jokes; but when reviewing his online recipe, it said, "the bag won't burn because paper burns at 451 degrees and we're at 375." I don't remember covering that scientific fact in any science class I had ever taken at Upper Iowa University, but there is a lot I don't remember from my days in school. Ah, what the hell, I thought. If this baby goes up in flames it won't be something we will soon forget. To tell you the truth, I even had my camera ready for some action shots of the kids pulling a fireball turkey out of the oven at any moment.

Before placing the covered turkey into the oven, the instructions called to sprinkle the bag all over with water. As you might have expected, the water intended for the turkey bag found its way onto each of the kids, on the walls, the ceiling, and the floor. Normally I would exercise my authoritative father skills to bring the dosing of water to a halt, but today it didn't seem to matter.

As the turkey went in the oven for four or five hours we enjoyed sitting together with the Green Bay Packers vs. Detroit Lions game on the television, the volume of the TV way too loud, and sharing each other's' company. Tony assumed his customary spot on the floor, pillow behind his head, watching the game and occasionally turning around to say something or scream at the players from the Lions as they incredibly lost 37-26.

A Thanksgiving of Mixed Feelings

It was a good day, but still, Tony wasn't the same, whatever "the same" might be. Seriously, how might any young man or woman be the same after attending the Oregon Youth ChalleNGe? He entered the program to learn NOT to be the same as when he entered four months prior. I just hoped that he hadn't lost his spirit and his personality.

I don't have much experience with horses, although we live in horse country, but I do know enough to understand there is a fine line in the discipline of teaching manners versus breaking the spirit of an animal. Can that same principle apply to humans? I believe so. The next few days might give us a better feel for what was going on with Tony or if I was just overreacting.

The meal was wonderful. It was so good to be together. Safe. Sound. As we finished and carried the dishes from the dining room to the kitchen, Tony asked if it was okay to go spend a few hours with his friends. I really had expected for him to stay home after Thanksgiving dinner and spend the entire day and evening with us, but I understood. We still had three full days to spend with him, Friday, Saturday, and Sunday.

Maybe we should have planned something more special than just spending time together sitting around the house and watching television. Coming home and trying to blend in again with family and friends had to be hard.

Stuck in my book of famous quotations are about a dozen quotes, not in the book, but scribbled on pieces of papers, "Going home is hard because it means revisiting the person you used to be." I failed to identify the source, just the quote. And it is true, isn't it? Coming home after being subjected to a whole new world and then trying to pick up where you left off just months earlier had to be scary and overwhelming. I mean, how could his friends understand what he had been through and was soon to achieve. Was his transformation going to be welcomed by his friends? It had to cause pause for him and fear.

Richie Norton, the bestselling author of *The Power of Starting Something Stupid*, said, "to escape fear, you have to go through it, not around it." Maybe the fear is what was so scary and overwhelming for Tony. As I know now, every cadet who comes home on break and eventually graduates from OYCP must "go through" the fear.

Think how you might react if your best friend left for a few months, only to return a completely new person. And if you were that new person, how long might it be before you conformed to your old habits and actions to blend back in? Think about your life. Have you ever conformed or made the decision not to go "through" the fear to be accepted, liked, and welcomed? Eric Hoffer, an American moral and social philosopher, the author and recipient of the Presidential Medal of Freedom said, "people will cling to an unsatisfactory way of life, rather than change in order to get something better, for fear of getting something worse."

We saw little of Tony the next three days. We had asked that he be home by eleven o'clock each night, and he arrived home right on time. When he would arrive home he generally just said hello and would say he was tired and was going to bed.

We allowed him to take advantage of the opportunity to sleep-in, and sleep in late he did. Not waking up, showering, and coming downstairs until just before noon. Man, this had to be a major departure than his required wake-up call at OYCP at 6:00 a.m. each morning.

It was on Sunday evening, the evening before Tony was required to check-in on Monday at 1400 hours (2 p.m.). Leann and I were both disappointed, frustrated, and concerned that Tony had spent so little time with us and said so little and when I tried to engage him he was very standoffish and noncommittal. We didn't push it, however. Both Nicole and Christiano had to return to school on Monday morning, so before going to bed they wished Tony well knowing that in less than a month he would be home.

A Thanksgiving of Mixed Feelings

Tony spent most of Monday finishing up his laundry and ironing some of his clothes to take back. Both Leann and I had taken Monday off work, as well, so we could help Tony with any last-minute needs and Leann, of course, making Tony a great lunch. While all this was going on I began to write a letter to send back with Tony, knowing that after returning to OYCP he might have some free time before bedtime. What could I say to let him know how important the next 23 days would be for him?

Tony,

I thought you might like something to read upon your return to school tonight. I know it was always a hard time for me when I returned to college after a stay at home for a few days. Perhaps you will have much to talk about with your buddies and the review of their stay at home and I am hoping when you have a minute you might welcome the note from your dad.

Thanks for finding some time to sit down with mom and me to talk about things…especially your future. I am sad that we weren't able to better communicate the past few days. I hope you will consider how we might communicate better when you come home after graduation. I propose that we schedule an appointment together when you get back. I am serious. Many marriage therapists suggest that couples schedule dates to meet each week to just focus, without outside interruption, on themselves. The appointment they set cannot be cancelled. The time is almost sacred. So, can we do that? Just you, me and mom. No Christiano. No Nicole…and no one else. How about Saturday, December 22nd at 10:00 a.m.? I will make sure nothing at work or with my agents gets in the way. Mom will do the same. Graduation is on

The Challenge

Wednesday, the 19th…so you will have a few days to get home and unwind first. Is it a date?

I know your time at OYCP has been the toughest thing you have ever done. I commend you for making it. I would never say I know what you or any of the cadets have gone through…because I have no idea. I have no idea about any pain you are feeling, fears you are facing, or doubts you may have. I have read that the most common reason people don't overcome the odds is because they haven't challenged themselves. That might have been true for you before the ChalleNGe…but not now.

You have already expressed your decision to take more risks and push more boundaries (by joining the Marine Corps.), and hopefully the skepticism you had in your own abilities to be successful have been dashed.

As you prepare to leave OYCP and begin a new life might I suggest what author John Maxwell refers to as his daily dozen. If you are able to live within his twelve daily suggestions you will excel.

1. *Choose and display the right attitudes.*
2. *Determine and act on important priorities.*
3. *Know and follow healthy guidelines.*
4. *Communicate with and care for your family.*
5. *Practice and develop good thinking.*
6. *Make and keep proper commitments.*
7. *Earn and properly manage finances.*
8. *Deepen and live out your faith.*
9. *Initiate and invest in solid relationships.*
10. *Plan for and model generosity.*
11. *Embrace and practice good values.*
12. *Seek and experience improvement.*

A Thanksgiving of Mixed Feelings

So, is it a date? Saturday, December 22nd? Have a great week and a fantastic next 23-days.

I love you,

Dad

20
THE 10 THINGS

You'll never find peace of mind until you listen to your heart.

George Michael

I couldn't shake the feeling that Tony was moving backward rather than forward. Just two days after returning to OYCP from Thanksgiving break, Tony sent both Leann and me two separate letters. And yes, the concern we both had about him while he was home showed up in the letters.

> *Dad,*
>
> *Not much to say today, but thank you so much for everything. It was so good to be home. I didn't mean to be so short the whole weekend. I had a lot of things on my mind. I promise it will get better when I get home. I love you all so much and I feel like an ass for not showing that. I'm sorry again. I love you and will write more tomorrow.*
>
> *Thank you,*
>
> *Tony*

And the next day Leann received a letter;

Dear Mom,

Before I get started, I want to say I love you and appreciate everything you do for me and I will always love you no matter what. I will always be there for you, like you have always been there for me. I know that sometimes I can be disrespectful and blow up. I am sorry. It has never been my intent to hurt you.

I want to take this chance to thank you for everything you have done for me. There are no words to express how thankful I am. All the times I have failed you, yet you were always there behind my back telling me "get up and try again!" All the times you were sitting in your chair and I was crying. You were my shoulder. Whenever I needed something you were there with the answer. Thank you.

These last five months have made me realize what I have and everything I took for granted. Mom, you are amazing and I am so thankful for everything. I could go on and on for pages, but I won't.

You are the one who kept me in the program here at OYCP. During pre-ChalleNGe (the first two weeks) I had every intent, every night to call home and quit… but I told myself I wouldn't because "Mom has seen me quit too many times and too many things and it is doubtful that I will be given a second chance."

So, I have nearly done it. I have made it through the homesickness. I have made it through the pain and I have made it through the school work and classes (with a 3.5 GPA).

So, thank you mom for being my mom and my best friend. I can't wait to get home and really show you what I have learned here at The Oregon Youth ChalleNGe!

I love you Mom. Thank you.

Tony

These two letters helped me realize why Tony had been so distant on Thanksgiving weekend. He was scared. Graduation was just weeks away and he would have to return to the real world. Once again, I tried to find the right words to help comfort and inspire him.

Just 19 days before Tony's graduation I wrote him a letter. I began with a quote from a blog titled, "Follow Your Destiny, Wherever It Leads You" by Vicki Silvers.

Tony,

There comes a time in your life when you realize that if you stand still, you will remain at that point forever. You realize that if you fall down and stay down, life will pass you by. Rather than wondering about or questioning the direction your life has taken, accept the fact that there is a path before you now. Shake off the whys and what ifs and rid yourself of confusion. Whatever was – is in the past. Whatever is – is what is important. The past is a brief reflection. The future is yet to be realized." Today is here, Tony.

Mark Twain said, "Twenty years from now you will be more disappointed by the things that you didn't do than by the ones you did do." So, throw off the bowlines (a knot used to tie up a boat). Sail away from safe harbor. Catch the trade winds in your sails. Explore. Dream. Discover.

Tony, for the past five months I have worked hard to find the words to inspire you. I have spent countless hours making sure every letter…everyday…would present a positive look at your future. I know I have failed many days…but I hope…I pray… that you have kept some of the thoughts in mind…and maybe even on paper somewhere. Maybe even journal. I hope that you find strength in other people's words too. Words are powerful. So are you…if you choose to be.

So, what is next for you" Are you going to explore, dream, and discover…. or will you choose to be ordinary? Don't be that disappointed person who in twenty years failed to implement all that you have learned this past five months. Do you realize just how important the next few months will be for you? You now will literally set the table for your future. Choose the direction you now go with purposeful thought and enduring conviction.

You have said many things to me over the past five months. You have spoken astonishingly from your heart. I have every word you have written to me, sometimes and most often, more times than you can imagine. I have felt every pain and I have shared in every happiness and success you expressed to me. I have spoken sincerely from my heart. Don't ever forget this written journey we have shared together. This is our story. Friends are important, but don't ever forget your family. All of us will be by your side always. Family is forever.

The Challenge

So now, just twenty days from graduation, are you understanding the significance of this. Do you understand what these past months have been all about?

I believe you do. However, if you do not you are in trouble. Plain and simple. Surely you understand that the past five months have not been about punishment, rather, the past five months have been about "the gift."

I have a favor to ask of you. Would you please write down the ten things you have learned over this past five-month period? What ten things might you put into action when you return home? You have been charged these past five months with mundane and rigorous activities, duties and training. You have learned to get up at an exact time and go to bed precisely when told. You have learned to make your bed and to make exactly as directed and expected. You have learned to sit a certain way at your desk, in the lunchroom and at presentations. You have learned when and how to speak to your superiors. You wear your clothes, shine your shoes, brush your teeth and cut your hair as ordered. So, when you leave the ChalleNGe which of those will continue to be a part of your life? How will you contribute to your family? Will you keep your promises to yourself?

And what do you expect from me? What will you expect from us? You are a different young man. I have seen it. I might like it. I might hate it.... but.... you are different you were just five months ago, Tony.

Here is the deal. All the information presented to you at the ChalleNGe has been presented to you and your entire class 34 in a very organized and systematic manner. OYCP has learned to repeat the same dynamic and disciplined program with each class. The food you have been given has been carefully planned and tested. The times that you get up in the morning and go to bed at night steadfast and tested. It was the same for the last class and will be repeated with the class after you. It works.

So, let me go first. I mean, with the ten things that "I" have learned the past five months. I mean, if it is fair for me to ask you to write down ten for me, then I should reciprocate with my ten. Right? Here goes:

1. *I have learned that being away from you makes my heart hurt. Literally.*
2. *I have learned that seeing your smile after a long absence overtakes my emotions and makes me magnificently happy.*
3. *I have learned you too have seen your potential realized.*
4. *I have learned for the past five months I have taken every opportunity to tell those I talk to about you.*
5. *I have learned over theses last five months that I have never been prouder of you.*
6. *I have learned that for the past five months, almost every day and night, I have awakened with my very first thought being of you…and fallen to sleep with my final thought being of you.*
7. *I have learned that you have proved to yourself that you are smart, passionate, purposeful, tenacious with a heart full of hope and now you have no more excuses to not be spectacular.*
8. *I have learned that I have missed you play ball.*
9. *I have learned, now more than ever, that time is precious and that every second counts.*

10. I have learned that you are becoming a man worthy of all your desire.

I love you,

Dad

I was hoping to break out of, what was many times, a one-way conversation with Tony. Often, I would ask him specific questions, and learned later that he would read my letters and would view my questions figuratively and not specifically. Honestly, I think it might be because he had never learned the simple art of letter writing. So, with this letter I had to try and make it clear that I was searching for his thoughts and answers.

Three days later I received a letter from Tony in direct response to mine.

Hey Pop,

Well, last night I read your letter from Friday, November 30th. It was all good until I got to the list at the end of your letter about the 10 things. Then I broke down, laid on the bed and cried. Shortly after that I fell asleep. That was some powerful stuff Dad…and I thank you for that.

I am so sorry for letting you down so much in the past. I really never realized how much you cared about me. I was stupid and that is something I never want to do again. So, after a lot of thought I will answer your questions as best as I can.

The 10 Things I will do when I get home:

The 10 Things

1. *I will make every attempt to be with my family.*
2. *I will take what I have learned here and use it in school.*
3. *I will make my very best effort to be with Yanno and help him with anything that I can.*
4. *I will never give up on anything.*
5. *I will stay away from drugs and alcohol.*
6. *I will work hard at any job I get.*
7. *I will love my family and contribute to them.*
8. *I will respect your house and pick up after myself.*
9. *I will go to church every Sunday.*
10. *I WILL BE HAPPY!*

And…the 10 Things I Have Learned At OYCP.

1. *I have learned that for once my family is proud of me.*
2. *I have learned to never quit on something you want.*
3. *I have learned that being away from my family hurts.*
4. *I have learned that I am not dumb and that I just need to apply myself.*
5. *I have learned that I am lucky to have the family that I do who love me so much.*
6. *I have learned that I love myself and have a lot of self-esteem.*
7. *I have learned how to prepare for the long road ahead.*
8. *I have learned that I have gained 45 brothers in 5 months.*
9. *I have learned that I am a leader.*
10. *I have learned that I am now a man.*

Love you,

Tony

As I read his words, "I have learned that I am now a man," I wondered exactly what that meant.

Obviously, you don't need to be a shrink to see how the lessons boys learn at the Youth ChalleNGe affect their behavior, but, a man? What does that mean? Does it mean that he can now admit that sometimes he needs help? Does it perhaps mean that he now realizes he is responsible for his own choices in achieving success in life? Will he follow blindly or have his eyes been opened up?

The truth is, perhaps like you, I know that I want for Tony to learn respect and honor. I know I want for him to treat all people kindly. I want for him to have an open and curious mind and heart. And I hope he finds the spiritual strength and guidance that only God can provide. Honestly, learning to become a man is a lifelong journey and I am hoping he is well on his way.

21
THE PRIZE

A real love letter is made of insight, understanding, and compassion. Otherwise it's not a love letter. A true love letter can produce a transformation in the other person, and therefore in the world. But before it produces a transformation in the other person, it has to produce a transformation within us. Some letters may take the whole of our lifetime to write.

Thích Nhất Hạnh

It was day 148, if I was counting correctly. Friday, December 14th, just 5 days from Tony graduating from OYCP and finally coming home.

Of all the letters, I wish to share with you, my final letter to Tony, for me, was the most significant. It was the easiest and it was the hardest to write. After hundreds of hours of putting pen to paper, finally my final letter to Tony while a cadet at The Oregon Youth ChalleNGe.

The Challenge

Tony,

This is it. This will be my last letter written to you while you are at the Oregon Youth ChalleNGe. Just a few days short of 5 1/2 months of letters.

In the time period from July 19th, we have spent just a few hours with you. I have missed that. We will never get that time back. It is gone and forever behind us.

I will never forget this experience, as I know you won't.

While I have not experienced YOUR feelings and I won't pretend to know what this past 5 months have been like for you...I can only reflect on those feelings I have personally experienced.

I want you to know my feelings because for you to know my feelings will make this experience more fulfilling for you, I believe.

Some 7 months ago, you walked into our home, well past curfew and received the thoughts of your family and the concern(s) we had for you. As we all sat and waited for you to come home that evening we contemplated what the results of our harsh and pointed conversation might bring. I can only speak from MY feelings. I won't pretend to know what your mother and Nici and Yanno felt that night. I know exactly how I felt. I want you to know. You must know.

That night was a life changing moment in our family. It was never to be the same. It will never be the same. It has changed my life. I know it has changed yours too.

My telling you that I wanted you to enter The Oregon Youth ChalleNGe was the most difficult words I can ever remember speaking. The fact is, I never really wanted you to go to OYCP. I never wanted to have you leave our home for more than 5 months. I hated myself for even suggesting it, for even thinking it. I mean, what kind of father tells his son that he needs to go away from home for 5 months for his senior year in high school? What kind of monster was I to take you away from school…from friends…from home? I have often wondered about that.

The fact is, I knew I had to do it. Mom agreed as she cried. Nici insisted that it was about you and not us. Yanno was heartbroken that such severe measures had to be taken to help you, but maybe he understood the best. I'm not sure.

I will never forget….and it still haunts me to this day and will perhaps every day for the remainder of my life. You, sitting next to me on the couch, your face down and in your hands and you repeating, "oh no, oh no, oh no." I can still see it. I can still hear it. How awful. How painful. As I spoke I hurt inside with every word I spoke to you…. but I knew I had to do it. Or did I? Perhaps I am about to find out.

So, as I write this letter…. the final letter to you as a cadet at the Oregon Youth ChalleNGe, I hope I did the right thing for you. I hope that the more than 3000 hours you have spent under the roof of the ChalleNGe has been the right thing for you.

I have missed you so much. You have no idea. Believe me.

The Challenge

Even in your absence, you have been the focus of my life. Not an hour has gone by for these 5 months that you have not been on my mind. The "things" that you left here have still been part of my every day, think about this for a moment. Here are just a few... off the top of my mind, ways, each day, that you have come to mind in my daily life for the past 140 plus days.

1. *Walking by your bedroom door several times a day.*
2. *Seeing the basketball hoop in front of the house each day.*
3. *Yanno wearing your clothes.*
4. *The basketball(s) on the front porch chairs.*
5. *Getting the garbage out each week.*
6. *Getting in mom's car and seeing the MV sticker and your old jersey number on her back window.*
7. *Working on the computer and seeing your pictures.*
8. *Coming to work and marking the day off my calendar.*
9. *Driving past MV High School.*
10. *Watching Yanno play ball and remembering my watching you from the time you were old enough to throw a ball and even thinking about your photograph wearing the Bears uniform.*
11. *Talking to Don and Joann and them asking about you or my telling them about you.*
12. *Seeing your friends in stores, at games or anywhere.*
13. *Your sweatshirts still hanging up in the closet and hallway.*
14. *When Nici does text messaging.*
15. *When I see Yanno play rough with Copper.*
16. *When I watch basketball, football, Nascar.*
17. *Every time I read the sports page.*
18. *When I read a book looking for thoughts that might help you.*

19. *When certain television shows are on.*
20. *When I go for a walk.*
21. *When I use the hair trimmer.*
22. *When I see ads anywhere for the military branches.*
23. *When I see a soldier.*
24. *Whenever there is any event in Bend where a security detail may need to assist.*
25. *When I see your hot sauce in the refrigerator.*
26. *When I go to the mailbox.*
27. *Before I go to the mailbox*
28. *After I go to the mailbox.*
29. *When the wind storm hit and I had to take the basketball set-up down.*
30. *When I had Nici move her car while one windstorm was blowing through and minutes later the basketball set-up blew over and just missed her car!*
31. *When I see the kids playing basketball in our neighborhood.*
32. *When I would see the goofy kid across the street walk in or*
33. *Walk out the front door.*
34. *When I hear loud music coming from cars.*
35. *When Yanno plays music on the computer in the kitchen.*
36. *When it was so hot and I thought you might be outside working or engaged in physical training.*
37. *When I would just drive out by the ChalleNGe to see if you might be running by or something.*
38. *Whenever I see a bag of Doritos in the pantry.*
39. *When I open the front closet, and see your caps.*
40. *When I clean up pee on and around the toilet.*
41. *When I do laundry and none of the clothes belong to you.*
42. *When I see the St. Louis Rams scores.*

43. When I watch Oregon games that I wish you could see too.
44. On the occasions where I might put on some cologne.
45. Whenever I adjust my seat for passengers in the back.
46. Whenever I walk up the front steps and remember you helping me stain and wonder if you did the steps where the stain is coming off.
47. Each time I eat a slice of cheese and unwrap it.
48. Every time I drive past Safeway.
49. Whenever I get extra change from the basket on top of the refrigerator.
50. Each time I see your shoes in the garage, which is every day at least twice.
51. Just about every time I look at Yanno and remember you at his age.
52. Every time I get a haircut.
53. Just about every time I eat and wonder what you had to eat.
54. When I drink a soda and think that you don't get soda.
55. When I see guys buy chew while I am waiting in line at the Butler Market store.
56. When it is cold and wondering if you are running outside and cold.
57. When I polish my shoes.
58. When I drive though Providence.
59. When we go out to eat at certain places.
60. When I go to bed early and don't have to worry about where you are.
61. When I read your letters in my green chair.
62. When no one has gotten the mail yet and someone comes home. "Hey, did you get the mail"
63. When I drive past car lots and see trucks you might like.
64. When I see cell phone ads.

65. When I pull up mom's foot rest on her chair.
66. When I walk on the street coming and going to MV.
67. When I see Pierce Kennedy in our neighborhood.
68. When I see a plane, and think about you considering the Air Force.
69. When I go to church.
70. When we make plans without you being in them.
71. When watching a Trailblazers highlight, thinking about what fun you and Yanno had at the game Uncle Don got great tickets for.
72. When I have gone to football games at MV and remembering you playing ball.
73. When I get gum out of the kitchen drawer.
74. When I see military bumper stickers.
75. When I write my affirmations, several times a week.
76. When I saw Craig Reid looking at the house across the street.
77. When I drive past Fargo Street (where Reid now lives).
78. When I have gone to the movies and know you haven't been to a big screen theatre in a long time.
79. Obviously, when your name comes up in our everyday conversations at home.
80. Whenever we go somewhere and can't invite you.
81. When my employees ask about you.
82. When we have looked at family video tapes.
83. When I have talked to people from Oelwein and your Uncle Dickie.
84. When I pray.
85. And even this very second, when Marie Phillis (from across the hall to my north) just came in and asked about you.

The list could go on and on.

The Challenge

Now thankfully, you are just hours from graduation from the Oregon Youth ChalleNGe. You are about to embark on a very difficult period in your life. Everything is in YOUR hands. It is up to you. You can choose to fail. You can choose to do great things. You do have it in you to do the great things, but you have to want it.

I will miss writing my letters to you each day. In a way, there will be an empty space in my daily routine that letters to you filled. But...hopefully, that empty space will be filled with many hours of having you home and just knowing you are just a few feet away.

Letters have allowed both of us to say the things we might not have ever said otherwise. The paper and pencil has, in many ways, set you free. Now, perhaps, you can see the reasoning for the letter writing at OYCP. There is nothing like the written word and the expression that comes out on paper. So...thank you for your letters. Thank you for sharing your sadness, tears, achievements, goals, concerns, pressures and happiness.

I consider the letters I have written to you "love letters" of a special kind. The kind only a parent can write. A great Zen scholar once said, "A real love letter is made of insight, understanding, and compassion. Otherwise it's not a love letter. A true love letter can produce a transformation in the other person, and therefore in the world. But before it produces a transformation in the other person, it has to produce a transformation within us. Some letters may take the whole of our lifetime to write."

You have done it! You promised yourself you would. You promised me that you would. You have lived up to your promises made. There is nothing as valuable in your life than meeting your commitments.

So, "the prize" is yours. You have done it, Tony. Now, it is time to maximize on what brought you to "the prize." Don't ever let yourself down again. Certainly, there will be small stones in the road. Know now that you can kick them aside as you move forward. With your head up and your chest out you have achieved what few have done or had the opportunity to accomplish....and there is nothing powerful enough to stop you.

I will miss writing to you. In a way, I hate the thought of knowing that you are no longer a captive audience for my daily letters and every word that I have spoken through them. But let's not be strangers.

Welcome home, Tony. I have missed you.

Love,

Your Dad

As I wrote this letter to Tony I wept. I recalled an interview I watched featuring American actor, Johnny Depp. He said "people cry, not because they are weak, but because they've been strong too long." I don't know if his wisdom applied to me, but it sure felt like it might.

22

GRADUATION DAY

*I'm not going to get somewhere and say, 'OK, I'm done.'
Success is never final; I'll just keep on going. The same way
as failure never being fatal. Just keep going. I'm going
to the stars and then past them.*

Conor McGregor

Finally, it was here...Graduation Day at the Oregon National Guard Youth ChalleNGe. We thought this day might never come,

While Tony was at the ChalleNGe I came across a book at our local library that has become a favorite of mine. Coincidently, a couple years after Tony's graduation from the ChalleNGe I received a personal copy of the book, *Critical Choices*, that had been signed by the author, Daniel R. Castro, and given to me by Exit Realty Corporation's, then president, Tami Bonnell. Tami Bonnell, today the CEO, heads one of the leading real estate franchises in the world, yet remembered my story of Tony and sent the book to me. I'm sure upon reading it herself she saw in its pages, pieces that would comfort and inspire me. One of my favorite quotes found in the book is from William Bridges, a noted author. He wrote:

Graduation Day

Whether you choose your change or not, there are unlived potentialities within you, interest and talents not yet explored. Transitions clear the ground for new growth. They drop the curtain so the stage can be set for a new scene. What is it, at this point in your life, that is waiting quietly backstage for an entrance cue?

I had written that quote on the back of an envelope of a letter I had sent to Tony just a few short months before sitting at his graduation. Would he realize, I wondered, that there was so much potential yet to be realized in his life? Would he find those talents given to him? How might he set the stage in his life for a new scene? Today, his graduation day certainly must be the cue from backstage.

The graduation was held at the Deschutes County Fairgrounds in a beautiful facility called the South Sisters Conference Hall and was set to begin at 11:00 a.m. The fairgrounds are about a 15-minute drive from our house, and a 20-minute commute from the OYCP facility, but we wanted to arrive early to secure a good seat.

Leann, Nicole, Christiano, and I all made arrangements to be at the graduation ceremony. Leann and I took a day off from work, Nicole took a personal day from her teaching position and Christiano was excused from attending school. It was a chilly morning, but for a mid-December day it was totally tolerable, sunny, and required only a light coat. One thing was for sure. Today was going to be a good day. A great day, in fact, and best of all, Tony would be coming home with us. This time for good!

When we arrived on the fairgrounds there was already a number of cars in the parking lot outside the main gates of the fairgrounds entrance. I imagined many had made the drive, as they did the first day they delivered their son or daughter to the ChalleNGe, from miles and hours away. Graduation at OYCP also brings out more than just the parents of the cadets. Family members, teachers, dignitaries, local press, and special guests are also part of the mix of attendees.

As we approached the door we took our place in a line maybe 100-deep. The disposition and the energy of those waiting in the line was a stark contrast from those that brought their children to the ChalleNGe on that first day of July. This day, instead of quiet, sad, and withdrawn faces, those waiting were laughing, smiling, and celebratory. What a difference, I thought.

The main door opened and we made our way inside to the hall. There were perhaps 400 chairs set up allowing for a wide aisle going down the middle. Towards the front, and slightly to the left, was a separate seating area that was reserved for staff, teachers, and others. The main stage was perhaps five feet high. There were two large video screens as well. The stage included a podium with perhaps four chairs on each side which were set back slightly, obviously reserved for those who would be special guests or speakers.

We looked over the seating area trying to decide the very best spot to see Tony as he would march in with his class. We decided on an area, maybe 20 rows from the front and slight stage right with an aisle seat. I wanted to have the flexibility to move quickly should a picture opportunity become available.

We sat and as I perused the program, I could see that the dignitaries in attendance included Brigadier General J. Michael Caldwell, the Oregon National Guard Deputy Director for State Affairs. There were familiar faces of some local politician, and walking near the front was Dr. Douglas Nelson, the Superintendent of the Bend School District whom I had spoken to directly so many months ago, asking, but never receiving his direct involvement in helping Tony at Mountain View High School. I thought briefly how I might not be here if Tony would have received the help I thought he so desperately deserved from our school district; but today was not a day to place blame, hold grudges, or look for people to blame. Oddly enough, Dr. Nelson was also the keynote speaker listed in the program.

I caught a glimpse of Marine Sergeant Tryon whom I had met earlier when attending career day at the ChalleNGe and spoke to about Tony's interest in the United States Marine Corps. He had Marine written all over him. The stereotypical Marine if I had ever seen one. He was a mountain of a man with biceps certainly formed by an extreme regime of exercise and dedication. His uniform fit tight and perfectly. Not a wrinkle in his clothing. I could understand why so many young men and women would be drawn to him when considering a career in the military. He was busy making the rounds talking to many people, doing his thing as you might imagine a recruiter does as part of his job.

I had never been to an Oregon Youth ChalleNGe Graduation Ceremony before, but this event had the same excitement and feeling of anticipation as any high school or college graduation I had ever been too, even more.

We sat and looked at the large video screen in front of us. Still pictures of the class showed different stages of the five and a half-month ChalleNGe. Occasionally, we were able to pick out Tony from all the other cadets who had their heads shaved almost the same as one another. Every once in a while, Christiano would grab my sleeve and say, "Hey dad! There's Tony!" as he was fixated on the screen.

The graduates were all placed in a smaller room to the back of the large hall, guarded and kept mostly out-of-sight, requiring attendees to twist and turn and sit and stand, trying to steal a look of their child. We would occasionally see the green cap and gowns of the graduates or the uniforms of those who are part of the drill team or color guard. Some of the cadets would stick their head out of the door with huge smiles, looking for their loved ones, and pointing their family members out to cadet friends at their side.

As 11:00 a.m. approached more activity began to take place near and on the stage. The seats were now mostly filled. The speakers and dignitaries had taken their place on stage and I saw Cadet Julio Linares walk up to the microphone. I remembered this young man because on the day of intake to the ChalleNGe I remember a big young man perhaps 50 pounds' overweight, maybe more, and wondering how he would ever make it through the high physical demands of the program. However, as he moved towards the podium, even with his graduation gown flowing down from the top of his shoulders to the floor, he looked like a different kid. Today he was looking confident, proud, and maybe 50 pounds lighter. His face thinner and his smile brighter. "Welcome!" he said with his big baritone voice. The hall, filled with conversation and laughter, quieted immediately. He proceeded to acknowledge special guests, thanking all who were in attendance and then he told his story.

He spoke of why he found his way to the ChalleNGe and how he was lost, but was found. His story was not much different than most kids who were graduating on this day or with previous classes. He spoke to how he decided enough was enough and how he worked hard to become the student body president and to graduate proudly from the ChalleNGe. I'm not sure there was a dry eye in the entire hall, including mine.

Upon Cadet Linares completing his welcome address and resuming his seat, Commandant Patrick Shields walked up to the podium, welcomed everyone, and asked the room to stand for the presentation of the colors. The colors were brought forward quietly and orderly by those OYCP students who were selected to be part of the color guard. They marched forward, in perfect step, to the stage, each taking a side to walk up and place the colors upon the stage. Of course, the American flag was placed to our left and the State of Oregon colors were placed to our right. At that time, we could look back and see the cadets, all in green and lining up to take their place in the seating area to the front. There were 122 graduates in all.

It is the same procedure that tens of millions of graduates have been part of, but this was Tony and 121 other young men and women who were given a second chance. Some of those who began the journey on the 19th of July didn't make it. It is that way with every class. More than twenty had left the program for personal reasons or had been sent home for not following the strict guidelines. They had been written off many months ago. Most would have likely not graduated from high school without this opportunity. This group and each graduating class learn that falling down, setbacks, losses, failures, and mistakes make up the obstacles on the road to success. Today was a success. The road ahead was wide open for each of them to travel.

Again, I felt a tug on my sleeve. Christiano had spotted Tony walking towards the front, slowly with perfect posture, standing well above most of his class, and with the "Tony Smile" ripping across his face from one ear to the other. Literally. After everything he had been through in his life, I thought how deserving he was to finally be recognized for completing, not just anything, but graduating from one of the toughest and finest youth programs in America.

As the "National Anthem" was presented by two of the programs graduating cadets, emotions gripped at me. I feared to look anywhere other than straight ahead for I might not be able to handle the tears coming from parents, grandparents, and family members who surrounded me. For the next more than an hour, we heard from the speakers and waited patiently for the presentation of the graduating class. Awards were distributed, those graduating with a GED were recognized and then it was time.

From the public-address-system we heard "Cadet Anthony James Mazziotti." Tony walked across the stage when his name was called, shook the hand of the presenter, received his diploma, and walked off and back to his seat. Joy consumed his beautiful face.

I sat as the remaining graduates were called to approach the stage and receive their diplomas. As their names were called I would look for their families and speculate and ponder what they were feeling and how this experience had changed their lives.

Shortly after the certificates and diplomas had been awarded to each cadet and other words of encouragement and congratulations were proclaimed, the class stood, turned and made their way to the back of the hall. Some made their way with smiles, others with tears. Tony looked towards us. There has never been a moment where he has looked prouder than this moment. This tiny little moment. This unbelievable moment.

As the last cadet made his way to complete the recessional, anxious parents and friends moved quickly to congratulate and celebrate with their graduate. I took just a few minutes to take it all in and to watch Tony hug the new friends he had made these past months. Once he was done, he clearly looked around him looking for us and once his eyes came in contact with ours his face gleamed. I can best describe what I saw in his face at that moment by using the words of poet, Julia C.R Dorr, "like the bright miracles we see in dreams." Yes, his faced gleamed like the bright miracles we see in dreams, for this was surely a miracle, the miracle I hoped for in every dream I have ever had for Tony.

When we finally were able to make our way through the crowd to greet one another I stood back to take it all in. First, he hugged and kissed his mother, then Nicole, and then a very excited Christiano. I simply stood back and took it all in. I thought about our journey and the letters. Yes, the letters. How they had changed my life and had likely changed Tony's life. Now, what would I do without the mission to write the letters to him? What would I continue to write and to whom?

The letter writing campaign had come to a close. Would I miss it? Surely, I would.

When it was my turn I placed my arms around him, looking up slightly, and said to him, "It is yours, Tony. The prize is yours. It has always been within reach. You just had to find it. I love you and I am so proud of you."

23
AFTERWORD

What every man/woman needs, regardless of his/her job or the kind of work he is doing, is a VISION of what his place is and may be. He needs an objective and a PURPOSE. He needs a feeling and a BELIEF that he has some worthwhile thing to do. What this is no one can tell him. It must be his own creation. Its success will be measured by the nature of his vision, what he has done to equip himself, and how well he has PERFORMED along the line of its development.

Joseph M. Dodge

Tony's story doesn't end here; it only begins. After leaving OYCP he returned to complete just one credit hour that he needed to receive his high school diploma from his high school, Mountain View High School. He wanted to be part of his MVHS class of 2008, and he did. Just a few months after he graduated from high school he entered the United States Marine Corps.

He has accomplished so much, first as a Marine who served in Afghanistan, and now he is a supervisor for a major Central Oregon landscaping company. He is a smart, productive, happy, and caring young man who someday hopes to have a family and a business of his own. We have The ChalleNGe to thank for that.

While Tony was a cadet at The Oregon Youth ChalleNGe, I sent 144 letters to him. 144 Letters To My Son. Joseph M. Dodge, an academic and economic advisor to President Eisenhower, once spoke of the needs of every man and women. They include vision, purpose, belief, and performance. I know Tony believes in and has his own VISION for the future. He believes there is a place for him. He recognizes his PURPOSE to do the very best he can to be a good son, an extraordinary friend, and to do great work, whatever that work may be. Yes, I know he has BELIEF in the most important thing in his life – himself. Lastly, I know he understands that life is made up of PERFORMANCES that will position him to achieve in life where he expects to, like a Champion, win with relationships, with learning, with jobs and always do so with honor and gratitude.

If you have a son or daughter who needs help, take whatever opportunities you have to raise them up. Find your way to do so. My way, I believe was with 144 letters that shared my heart to my son and some of them, now, with you. The thought of writing letters to my son began days before he left home and entered The Oregon Youth ChalleNGe. Shortly before he left I looked at a calendar provided in his entrance materials for The ChalleNGe. As I looked I thought, "why not write each day to Tony? Let's see, it looks like the calendar is about 150 days? Yep, I can do this. I will do this," I said to myself. And as I write to him I will be sure to express a reoccurring theme and goal throughout each letter. I wrote those goals down and put them on a wall next to my desk in my office. It was there where I would write each letter and each day.

My 5 Goals of Letter Writing While Tony Is Away

1. Reaffirm each day how proud of him that both my family and I are of him and his assertiveness and commitment to complete The Oregon Youth ChalleNGe.

2. To build each letter with inspirational quotes and the powerful words of others to help him identify what is possible to ensure that he: recognizes he has purpose, that he is relevant, and that he is loved by God and his family.

3. That he can accomplish this.

4. Nothing can stop him achieving success.

5. Our entire family and I are there with him now, during, and after his completion of the Oregon Youth ChalleNGe Program.

So even, on any given day, and when I may have little to say, I would do my very best to inspire him to reach beyond what he thought possible.

Johann Wolfgang von Goethe, the German writer who filled the eighteenth century with his writings said:

Things that matter most must never be at the mercy of things that matter least.

My goal would be to live in the words that Goethe and others wrote about. Those beautiful words have so inspired me and I know inspired Tony, too. To this day he keeps the torn remains from the back of envelopes where I had written quotes just after placing a letter inside and after sealing each letter. The quotes, the words, and the letters changed us both, forever. Words written on paper can change your life and those who receive your words; but first you must find the words. My words came from my heart, from my tears, from my anguish, and from my pain. My words came from many others, too. I am so appreciative for the words and I owe so much to The 144 Letters To My Son.

FINAL THOUGHTS

BE THE BRIGHTEST LIGHT FOR YOUR CHILD

One of my favorite authors is Jon Gordon. He has written several inspirational books that I use regularly with my team of agents at Exit Realty and I used in one letter that I sent to Tony.

The story that Jon Gordon tells goes like this:

As I ran to the beach the other day I noticed certain areas were closed off by fences and signs that said, "Sea Turtle Eggs."

I remembered reading that female sea turtles swim to shore between May and August to dig nests in the sand and lay their eggs. Months later, the eggs hatch and the baby turtles follow the pure light of the moon back to the surf.

In a perfect world, the pure light of the moon guides every turtle back safely to the ocean. However, as we know, we don't live in a perfect world.

Sea Turtle hatchlings instinctively crawl toward the brightest light. On an undeveloped beach, the brightest light is the moon. On a developed beach, the brightest light can be an artificial light source emerging from restaurants, homes, and condominiums along the coast.

Unfortunately, these powerful light sources of light often attract the hatchlings and cause them to move in the wrong direction when they are born.

Rather than follow the pure light of the moon to the ocean the sea turtles follow the wrong light to a disastrous outcome.

It occurred to me that we humans face a similar challenge.

Rather than follow the path we are meant to follow, unfortunately we too often are distracted by things that move us in the wrong direction.

Technology, online games, too much time on social media, bad habits, addictions, stress, business, and meaningless distractions lead us astray.

Instead of following the pure light of perfection we allow bright and shiny artificial things to sabotage our journey.

So what about you?

Are you following your priorities and pure light to the right destination or are you allowing artificial distractions to lead you in the wrong direction?

Are you following the path you were meant to follow or are you letting meaningless things keep you from being your best?

The great news is that unlike sea turtles we have the ability to think, adapt and change direction when we realize we are following the wrong path.

FINAL THOUGHTS

We can tune out the distractions and focus our priorities and let the pure light lead us to an ocean of possibilities and a great future.

I end with a class credo, drawn by the First Platoon Wolverines, Tony's Platoon at The ChalleNGe. I believe the words sum it all up. It addresses the mission of each family who strives to discover new beginnings for their children and for each member of every family that is a part of The ChalleNGe.

FIRST PLATOON WOLVERINES

The change is complete. We who came to OYCP in the search of self-worth and to replace confusion with meaning. All that was torn is whole again. And we stand in formation, as brothers, proud and loyal. From here we go with a purpose and we go as family. We have not yet reached a destination, but we have chosen a path, and that is a start. We have proven to ourselves that we can do more than any of us thought possible and we know this is our time to change the world, this is our calling. In the shining moment everything is possible, yet nothing written, perhaps that is the most exciting thing of all.

We came as wanderers. We depart as family.

First Platoon Wolverines
OYCP Class 34
July 19th-December 19th.
First Platoon Wolverines

The ChalleNGe continues to change the lives of kids in 40 Youth ChalleNGe Programs across the U.S.

ACKNOWLEDGMENTS

I met with Tony's former teacher, Joe Padilla, in preparation for this book. I could still see the qualities in this man that my son had seen as his high school instructor years earlier.

As he greeted me for lunch he wrapped his hand around mine firmly and confidently. Since having Tony in his classroom as a sophomore, he has moved on to another school teaching, and as head football coach placed in charge of turning around a high school program that has been the doormat of its football conference for forever (*by the way, Joe Padilla led the Bend, Oregon, Summit High School Storm football team to a state championship in 2015 as its head coach*).

As we spoke his eyes left mine just several times as he tried to recall the time and events he spent with Tony. He shared with me the frustration he felt when he worked with Tony in the classroom, not knowing what he was going to find on any given day. "Tony was a loose cannon, no question," he said. I asked him if Tony's impulsiveness was a factor. "Impulsiveness is the right word," he said. "Tony would act and then consider what action he had just taken, instead of the other way around," Joe continued. "He would realize what he did and acknowledge it, but I would frequently be required to ask him to leave my room, have him go sit in the hall for disrupting my classroom. When I would go out to the hall to check on him he would seldom be agitated and almost always took responsibility for his actions; but nevertheless, would repeat his behaviors often." He said, "Tony was a frustrated young man. He often spoke of how he knew he was letting you down by not excelling in school and sports, but it was clear he just couldn't find the pathway to do something about it."

Tony respected Joe so much that in the spring of 2007 and just after making his application to the Oregon Youth ChalleNGe Program, he asked Joe to be his personal mentor. You see, the Youth ChalleNGe Program requires each applicant to name a mentor in the application and before coming to the ChalleNGe. The ChalleNGe does not end after the intensive five and a half-month residency at the facility. The requirements of Youth ChalleNGe are that each cadet continue working with a mentor for an additional 12-month post-residential phase after leaving. The mentorship required that Joe maintain weekly contact for the duration (17 ½-months) of the program. In doing so, the mentor is in place as a person, outside of family, who assists with clearly defined standards, goals, objectives, and outcomes for each participant.

Joe spoke of how Tony took immense pride whenever he visited the facility. "He would show me where he ate, slept, and where he attended class each day with a sense of a newly found confidence, something he lacked before coming to The ChalleNGe. I could see the difference that the clearly defined expectations of each cadet played out for Tony. Finally, I thought, he was at a school with a firm structure that was there to focus on him and help develop a positive attitude and a successful outcome. This school was perfect for Tony," he concluded.

Many books have been written that have inspired me. One such book that has inspired me was written by the late Frosty Westering. Frosty was a longtime head football coach at Parsons College (located not too far from where I grew up) in Fairfield Iowa, Lea College in Albert Lea, Minnesota and finally at Pacific Lutheran University in Tacoma, Washington. He coached Pacific Lutheran football for 31-years, winning four national titles and assembled a combined college coaching record of 305-96-7, a NAIA record for the most coaching wins among all college football coaches. While coaching at Pacific Lutheran he never had a losing record for any season. He was inducted into the College Football Hall of fame in 2005. His book, *Make the Big Time Where You Are* being a testament to the man he was and the difference he made in young men's lives. He made his own big time by changing lives wherever he coached and did so by motivating his players. Frosty said, "People are motivated in basically three ways: fear, incentive and love. Fear and incentive are motivators that can produce quick results but soon they lose their effectiveness. They are both extrinsic and motivate from the outside rather than from within. Fear motivation is the old 'Kick in the Pants' stuff. In other words, if you don't do it, you get kicked in the pants. Further, he said, Love is a basic need of everyone - a genuine unselfish love that puts a priority on relationship and develops a healthy resilient rapport among people."

It is with his beliefs of motivation: fear, incentives, and love that speaks to me. So much so, that I ended up writing 144 letters in a span of just 154 days to my son while he was on the most incredible journey of his young life. The letters I share in this book represent just a few of the many letters that I wrote to Tony and those that he wrote to me. And I can't emphasize enough the importance of having the support of others - both family and friends. Letters, cards, and postcards all were major influences and offered support to Tony.

My sister, Joann and her son, Tony's cousin, Sam, for example sent Tony a variety of postcards based on a variety of "Iowa" themes. Before moving to Bend in 2002, and to this day, our family remains loyal University of Iowa sports fans, especially Tony. Tony attended a number of sport camps in his early years while in Iowa including his favorite with the Iowa Hawkeye basketball team camp. The saying, "you can take the kid out of Iowa, but you can't take Iowa out of the kid" applied to Tony. Most of Joann's postcards were "tongue and cheek" cards featuring iconic Iowa symbolism. One card featured a photograph and instructions on how to escape an Iowa tornado, another (actually two) featured photographs of Iowa hogs (by the way, Iowa far outpaces all other states in gross state production of more than 4-billion a year). One card with a gigantic ear of corn about the size of a house and, of course, Iowa Hawkeye cards with the famous tigerhawk logo. True to Iowa's history and reputation, the cards featuring hogs, corn, and football were probably spot on. I know they brought a smile to Tony's face.

My only brother, Don, 9 years my elder, the "Godfather" of our family, if one did truly exist, also supported Tony. In his letters, he reflected on his personal experiences that might have helped Tony see the light from another direction and from another's perspective. Don supported me as well. He has always supported me in anything I have ever done.

Certainly, there were friends of our family, cousins, aunts and uncles and others who made sure Tony knew that he was in their thoughts and prayers. Some, who I am sure he had hoped might offer him encouragement and support, weren't there, but we live in a very busy world. He understood, I understood. How many times, I have thought to myself, I didn't find the time to reach out to someone who could have used a helping hand or the right words to help provide them with the strength they may have needed in their time of crisis or need? Isn't it true that we know "things that matter most must never be at the mercy of things that matter least." I can do better. You can do better too. Honestly, what matters more than family, friends, and those whose friendships are held closely to your heart.

And how could I not acknowledge Tony's two siblings, Nicole and Christiano. Nicole and Christiano wrote many letters to Tony. I counted at least thirty letters that Tony brought home from the ChalleNGe that came to him from his brother and sister. I am guessing there were even more. Like most of my letters, their letters served as a vessel, transporting their love and support than that of delivering pertinent and important news from home. I think it would be safe to say that letters are like people in that they'll arrive at a time in your life when you most need them; for Tony and the cadets around him I know this held true. Nicole and Christiano are an amazing sister and brother. I love them so much.

And then there is Leann, my wife and Tony's mother. We have shared so much joy. We have always wiped tears from one another's face. No journey with a son or daughter is easy, and this journey with Tony has molded us to who we are, hopefully better and more loving than ever. I love you, Leann.

Finally, I want to thank the many people who have made such a significant difference in the life of Tony and me.

To Cadre Larry Demarr, thank you for guiding our son with a firm hand and a loving heart. You are making a difference in the lives of thousands of young men and women and their families. We shall, forever, be thankful you came into our lives.

To Dan Radabaugh, the Director of the OYCP, thank you for your leadership in helping make the Oregon Youth Challenge one of the finest facilities in the country and helping change the lives for thousands of kids in Oregon.

To Karen Rawnsley, the Deputy Director of OYCP, your kindness will always be remembered and appreciated. Thank you for encouraging me to submit an application for my son to attend the ChalleNGe.

To Frank Strupith, the Admissions Counselor for the OYCP, thank you for helping the youth of Oregon find a place where they can achieve success and realize their full potential.

To the Oregon Youth ChalleNGe teachers and staff, know that you make a difference in the lives of so many.

To Chris Stokes, a former instructor at the Central Oregon Intergovernmental Council's Alternative Education Program

(COIC), thank you for being a positive role model for Tony while he was a student at COIC. You made a difference.

Proverbs 22:6 tells us, "start children off on the way they should go, and even when they are old they will not turn from it." To the elementary teachers and nuns at Sacred Heart School in Oelwein, Iowa, who always worked tirelessly to guide Tony to be a caring and loving boy, starting Tony off on the way he should go and to always be the best student he could be, my deepest thanks.

To my writing coach, Linden Gross, your guidance helped inspire and motivate me. Thank you for being an amazing writing coach, a caring teacher, and a good friend.

To my developmental editor, Michele Stanford, thank you for your guidance.

To my graphic designer, Debbie O'Byrne, thank you for bringing my cover design to life.

To The National Guard Youth Foundation, thank you for your belief in second chances.

Joe Padilla, a fine man who accepted Tony's request to be his mentor, also wrote. Like all volunteer mentors who make a major investment in the students they mentor, I know Tony appreciated the time and effort Joe put into his mentoring Tony. When I reviewed Tony's letters I found a special one that Joe Padillia had sent to Tony and signed. It reads:

Mentor's Hope

I will strive to be a good role model.
I will listen to you with my heart as well as my ears.
I will use the benefit of my experience to guide you.
I will challenge you to find your passion.
I will help you recognize opportunity.
I will find the best in you.
I will respect your opinion.
I will set limits.

Acknowledgments

I will guide but not control.
I will focus on your strengths.
I will encourage responsibility in you.
I will provide support and not dependence.
I will recast problems as learning experiences.
I will be your friend.

The ChalleNGe Story

DOES NOT END HERE

www.thechallengestory.com

EXPERIENCE TONY'S JOURNEY THRU PICTURES & VIDEO
BEFORE The ChalleNGe
DURING The ChalleNGe
AFTER The ChalleNGe
And TODAY

LEARN HOW YOU CAN EXPERIENCE PERSONAL SUCCESS & overpower YOUR CHALLENGES

THE Challenge PODCAST
Conquer The Greatest Challenge Of All
Hear it On
Spreaker

The DREAM MAP

Discovery

A LIFE CHANGING PRESENTATION EVENT

LET'S MAP YOUR JOURNEY

- Create Your Dream Map
- Discover The 5 Roadblocks Preventing You To Dream
- Prepare For Dreaming
- Take The Dream Test
- Experience Your Maiden Flight & Soar With Eagles

Those interested may email Jim Mazziotti directly at soarwithexit@gmail.com or by calling 541-480-8835. Jim Mazziotti is available for customized presentations across America

bring JIM MAZZIOTTI
Author, Speaker, Coach & Trainer

to your event

GROW YOUR BUSINESS & TRANSFORM YOUR LIFE NOW!

PRIVATE, GROUP & MASTERMIND EVENTS

CORPORATE ENTREPRENEURSHIP AND LEADERSHIP TRAINING

EMPOWERING
MOTIVATING
TRANSFORMATIONAL

The JOHN MAXWELL Team

CPSIA information can be obtained
at www.ICGtesting.com
Printed in the USA
FSHW010610121019
62911FS